First, They Erased Our Name

Habiburahman, known as Habib, is a Rohingya. Born in 1979 in Burma (now Myanmar), he escaped torture, persecution, and detention in his country, fleeing first to neighbouring countries in Southeast Asia, where he faced further discrimination and violence, and then, in December 2009, to Australia, by boat. Habib spent 32 months in detention centres before being released. He now lives in Melbourne. Today, he remains stateless, unable to benefit from his full human rights. Habib founded the Australian Burmese Rohingya Organization (ABRO) to advocate for his people back in Myanmar and for his community. He is also a translator and social worker, the casual support service co-ordinator at Refugees, Survivors and Ex-Detainees (RISE), and the secretary of the international Rohingya organisation Arakan Rohingya National Organisation (ARNO), based in the UK. In 2019, he was made a Refugee Ambassador in Australia. The hardship and the human rights violation Habib has faced have made him both a spokesperson for his people and a target for detractors of the Rohingya cause.

Sophie Ansel is a French journalist, author, and director, who lived in South Asia for several years. It was during a five-month stay in Myanmar that she first encountered the Rohingya people and heard of their plight. She returned to the country several times, and also visited the refugee communities in neighbouring countries like Thailand and Malaysia, where she met Habib in 2006. Habib helped Sophie to better understand the persecution faced by the Rohingya, and she has been advocating for their cause since 2011. When the Myanmar government accelerated the genocide of the Rohingya in June 2012, while Habib was detained in Australia, she helped him to write his story, and the story of his people.

Andrea Reece is a translator of novels, short stories, and works of non-fiction from French and Spanish.

First, They Erased Our Name

A ROHINGYA SPEAKS

Habiburahman
with Sophie Ansel

Translated by Andrea Reece

SCRIBE
Melbourne • London

Scribe Publications
2 John St, Clerkenwell, London, WC1N 2ES, United Kingdom
18–20 Edward St, Brunswick, Victoria 3056, Australia
3754 Pleasant Ave, Suite 100, Minneapolis, Minnesota 55409 USA

First published in English by Scribe in 2019

Originally published in French as *D'abord, ils ont effacé notre nom* © Editions de la
Martinière, une marque de la société EDLM, Paris, 2018

This edition published by special arrangement with EDLM in conjunction with
their duly appointed agent 2 Seas Literary Agency

Supported using public funding by

**ARTS COUNCIL
ENGLAND**

This book has been selected to receive financial assistance from English PEN's
PEN Translates programme, supported by Arts Council England. English PEN
exists to promote literature and our understanding of it, to uphold writers'
freedoms around the world, to campaign against the persecution and imprisonment
of writers for stating their views, and to promote the friendly co-operation of
writers and the free exchange of ideas. www.english.pen.org

Typeset in 11/17pt Meno Text by the publishers
Printed and bound in the UK by CPI Group (UK) Ltd, Croydon CR0 4YY

Scribe Publications is committed to the sustainable use of natural resources and
the use of paper products made responsibly from those resources.

9781912854035 (UK edition)
9781947534858 (US edition)
9781925849110 (Australian edition)
9781925693720 (e-book)

Catalogue records for this book are available from the National Library of
Australia and the British Library.

scribepublications.co.uk
scribepublications.com
scribepublications.com.au

To the Rohingya,
To the memory of those whose blood continues to flow
into the soil of Arakan.

To all the weary stateless people who have fled and still roam
the oceans, jungles, and highways of the world,
hoping to survive.

To you, the reader, may you tell our story,
which has been stifled by propaganda, racism, fascism,
and deadly hatred.

May the truth one day be known and a light shone
on our tragedy, the hidden history of Burma.

To my family, to my father and my mother,
To tolerance and peace,
To life and love.

This book is not only my story.
It is the chronicle of a genocide.

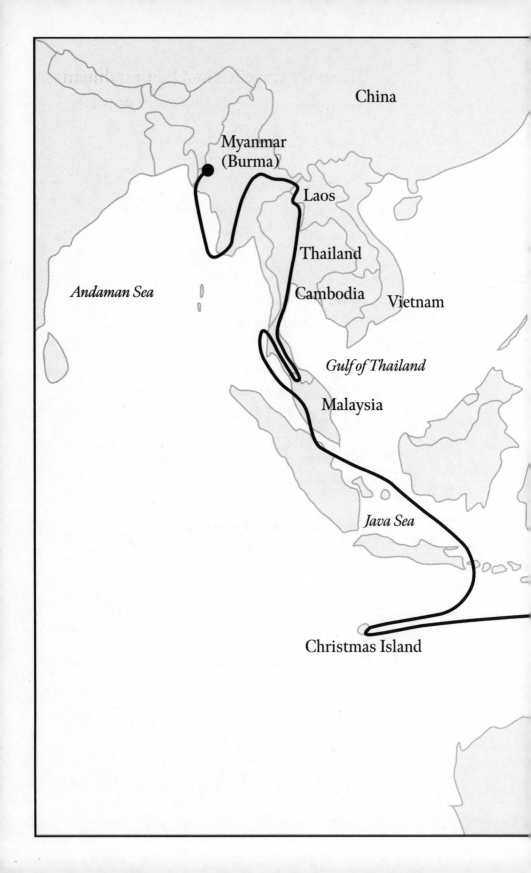

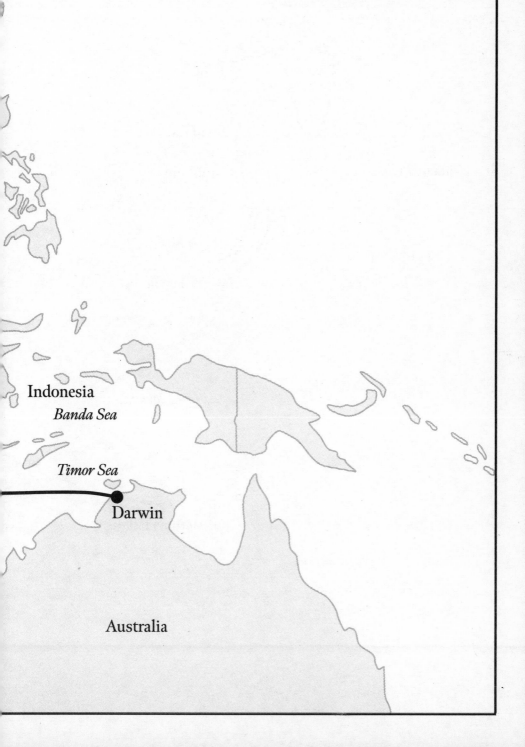

Itinerary travelled by Habiburahman
between 1994 and 2013

Indonesia

Banda Sea

Timor Sea

Darwin

Australia

1

The ogre of Burma is born

The dictator U Ne Win has presided over a reign of terror in Burma for decades. In 1982, he has a new project. He is planning to redefine national identity and fabricate an enemy to fuel fear. A new law comes into force. Henceforth, to retain Burmese citizenship, you must belong to one of the 135 recognised ethnic groups, which form part of eight 'national races'. The Rohingya are not among them. With a stroke of the pen, our ethnic group officially disappears. The announcement falls like a thunderbolt on more than a million Rohingya who live in Arakan State, our ancestral land in western Burma. The brainwashing starts. Rumours and alarm spread insidiously from village to village. From now on, the word 'Rohingya' is prohibited. It no longer exists. We no longer exist.

I am three years old and am effectively erased from existence. I become a foreigner to my neighbours: they believe that we are Bengali invaders who have entered their country illegally and now threaten to overrun it. They call us *kalars*, a pejorative term expressing scorn and disgust for dark-skinned ethnic groups. In a different time and place, under different circumstances, *kalar* would have meant wog or nigger. The word is like a slap in the face; it undermines us more with each passing day. An outlandish tale takes root by firesides in thatched huts across Burma. They say that because of our physical appearance we are evil ogres from a faraway land, more animal than human. This image persists, haunting the thoughts of adults and the nightmares of children.

I am three years old and will have to grow up with the hostility of others. I am already an outlaw in my own country, an outlaw in the world. I am three years old, and don't yet know that I am stateless. A tyrant leant over my cradle and traced a destiny for me that will be hard to avoid: I will either be a fugitive or I won't exist at all.

2

Grandma's stories

1984

In the candlelit glow of the hut, I half open my eyes through heavy eyelids and see Grandma's wrinkled and kindly face. Her features are blurred by the steam from the pot that she is stirring. The smell of rice and the crackling fire rouse me from my torpor. Grandma comes over and sits down cross-legged on the large grass mat that covers the mud floor. She wraps her arms around me and mops my burning forehead with a wet cloth scented with herbs that Dad has gathered in the forest. Next to her, Mum hums a barely audible tune as she rocks my little sister Nojum who is latched firmly on to her breast. Grandma lifts a spoonful of broth to my mouth. I close my eyes again, exhausted by illness. Her voice resonates like a distant echo: 'Keep going, little Habib. Drink this down and it'll make you strong again. A slight fever like this isn't going to finish you off. Be brave, my little one.'

Her words continue uninterrupted, barely distinguishable from the ambient noise. I don't know whether she is talking to me, Mum or Dad, or to the tormented figures from another time and place who live on in the depths of her memory. Fleeing, endlessly roaming, shrieking and screaming for help. The ghosts of our family and of our people who perished, decapitated by swords or burnt to death. This is where my fear of fire started: back then, the flames were always populated by Grandma's wailing ghosts.

She nuzzles into the hollow of my neck — a sign of infinite affection — and her voice pulls me back from sleep, into the story of our cursed people.

'Beyond the Kaladan River, there are far greater dangers than a touch of malaria, my little one. You're going to get better very quickly, and soon you'll be big enough to help your dad in his shop. You're safe here. Our village is still a peaceful oasis in this desert of hatred. They won't come looking for us here.'

She sighs. That drawn-out sigh that punctuates her often tedious tales. Never-ending stories that are always accompanied by a moral lesson and prayers to God, a burdensome chore that she drums into us on a daily basis when all my brother Babuli and I want to do is play.

Grandma's entire past is in her head, far removed from us, and it has the unfortunate habit of interrupting our giggling fits and spoiling our games. On this June evening just before the onset of the rainy season, I am too weak to break free and run off tittering with Babuli to our hideout behind the chicken coop, so I let myself be tenderly rocked to the melody of Grandma's husky voice and the gentle rhythmic movement of her shoulders. I watch as she drifts away. Her eyes cloud over and her gaze is fixed somewhere in the distance. Even before she opens her mouth, I know that the images in her head are back.

'A long time ago, Habib, the world was vast and infinite. Men and women travelled slowly, keeping time with nature and God as they searched for peaceful and fertile lands. Entire peoples boarded huge ships and crossed oceans. Sailors invoked the clemency of nature by offering up a small gem each day that was swallowed by the waves and deposited on the ocean bed. This is how our ancestors arrived safe and sound in the Kingdom of Rohang, which we now call Arakan. It is this land of plenty, blessed by God, which gave rise to the Rohingya, a peaceful tribe of fishermen and farmers.'

As if seeking his approval, Grandma turns towards Dad, who is busy scratching letters and figures into a notebook with yellowing pages. She continues her story: 'Our history has become both a lie and a crime in the eyes of the dictatorship. Their hatred and racism have turned us into foreigners who must be crushed.'

She squashes her nose into my cheek, inhales deeply, then places a clean cloth on my forehead, which is beaded with sweat.

'Your memory is all you will have to keep our history alive, Habib. So listen to me carefully, because your grandmother won't be here forever.'

I'm familiar with the history of the Rohingya. It's a nightmarish saga that Grandma recounts every evening.

'All I have to bequeath to you now are my words, my little man. We have been plundered of all our wealth. I was young, the same age as your mother, when they came and attacked our village, a few miles from here. They wanted to kill the Muslim *kalars*, they said. They stormed our homes and invaded

5

neighbouring villages. They overran the whole state. Swords swished through the air. Heads rolled. Women experienced torture that only they can know. Caught in a trap, some preferred to jump into the water and drown themselves rather than fall into the repulsive criminal hands of these men. We left our fields, goats, oxen, and hens. For days we fled through the forest along the border. This was in 1942.'

Dad finally looks up from his notebook and interrupts Grandma's flow: 'Mother, don't you think that he's too young to understand all that? You're going to traumatise him.'

Grandma falls silent, but the floodgates of her heart have opened. She won't leave it there.

She picks up a thanaka stick and vigorously grates the bark on the *kyauk pyin*†. After a few minutes, she extracts a cool yellow paste and gently applies it to my burning face. Out of the corner of my eye, I catch a glimpse of Babuli's silhouette. He is playing with stones on the mud floor. My desire to join him gives me renewed energy. I turn my head and stretch my arm towards him as I try in vain to escape Grandma's tight embrace. The malaria has drained me of all my strength. Sweat pours off me. Grandma keeps mopping. I give in.

'My son, who knows how long we have before we are chased away again?' Grandma starts up again, her words directed at Dad. 'What kind of luck have I had? My life has been defined by the loss of my loved ones. How many pogroms will there be before we are all annihilated? They took my father, they threw my husband in prison. God knows what they made him endure before he died. The Kaladan River runs red with our blood. God protect you for as long as possible. Your children must prepare themselves for the worst.'

---

† A flat circular stone.

Grandma shudders. She loosens her grip. My body slides into the gap between her legs and is caught by her flowery *longyi*†. A warm tear splashes onto my cheek from above as my head rolls back onto her knees. She recovers her composure, hugs me to her chest, and gives me a long, searching look. My father, immersed again in his notebook, is no longer listening.

Undeterred, she carries on telling me the secret and unwritten history of the Rohingya. After my grandfather's arrest in 1967, the massacres began again in earnest. The Rohingya had no choice but to flee to Bangladesh. They lived there in appalling and inhumane conditions until the first signs of a lull appeared in Burma. One of my uncles was too traumatised to ever return and chose exile in the Arab states with hundreds of thousands of other refugees. He was never seen again.

Once our people had left the country, it was difficult to return and reclaim what was rightfully ours. The authorities had robbed my family of everything, but my grandparents and my father had carefully conserved our title deeds. Arakan was the only possible place they could settle and find food and water, the only place they could hope to have a life.

In 1969, after a year roaming Bangladesh, suffering greatly, my family returned with a handful of other Rohingya to Biramno, their native village in a remote part of Kyauktaw Township. All their animals had been stolen, of course, but my grandmother hoped to be able to farm our land again. Unfortunately, it had been confiscated and redistributed. My father bravely approached the local authorities to claim what rightfully belonged to the family. He brandished the title deeds with great conviction. They arrested and tortured him. He

---

† Traditional Burmese dress consisting of a calf-length piece of fabric tied around the waist.

wrote to the federal government, which eventually conceded half of our original land. When others who coveted the land heard what had happened, the local authorities issued orders for my father to be killed. He had no choice but to flee once again with my mother. They took refuge in neighbouring Chin State. That is where I was born, in this remote and tolerant village by the Kaladan River, where different minorities live more or less in harmony. I was still in my mother's belly when the army chiefs launched another massive cleansing operation in 1978. They called it Operation *Nagamin* (Dragon King).

Grandma mutters. Her lips tremble and her eyes shine.

'They arrested hundreds of Rohingya and forced them onto makeshift boats. The boats were escorted to the middle of Sittwe Bay and sunk. Men, women, and children, all engulfed by the water. Then came the rapes, massacres, and imprisonments in Buthidaung and Maungdaw. The central government sent more boats to Kyauktaw, where I lived. The soldiers and extremists continued the house-to-house raids.'

Grandma says nothing for a few long minutes and then starts softly singing sad gentle words, accompanied by the crackling of the fire: '*The Dragon King will carry you off. Poor people, poor Rohingya ...*'

She rallies, and strokes my cheeks with the back of her dry, beat-up old hands.

'You are adorable, my little Habib. I love you so much. But the Burmese regime find your lovely ebony skin, your thick head of hair, and your beautiful dark eyebrows offensive. They see you as too black. Too Muslim. Too Negro. Too different. A parasite, like the rest of us. They prefer to confine us to tiny spaces, ghettos where they can control and trample us underfoot, reduce us to slavery, humiliate us, and spill our blood. They are orchestrating our disappearance and we can do nothing to stop them.'

Some Rohingya who lived in the smaller, more remote villages were warned about the Dragon King operations. My grandmother had just enough time to bundle up her most precious belongings, gather together her personal documents, and dig a deep hole under her hut in which to hide her life's savings: gold jewellery that she could not take with her. She chased her livestock into the woods and took a boat upriver, as far away as possible from the Arakanese militia. Those who refused to leave their homes were slaughtered or arrested and tortured. The extremists looted whatever they could. Hundreds of Rohingya were left dead. Thousands were imprisoned. Maybe more. Who knows? Who will ever care? Who will record the truth of such horrors? She fled for seven days until she arrived here and was taken in by my father. Months later, when she finally dared return to her home, she had lost her land, her livestock, and her gold. In barely three months, the countryside had been emptied of hundreds of thousands of Rohingya who were reduced to roaming Bangladesh in indescribable conditions. Fleeing. Always fleeing.

Tiredness overcomes me. All I can hear is vague murmuring. I doze off, warmed by the flames of the fire. The fragrance of the jasmine flowers hanging from the bamboo wall comforts me and sets me to dreaming, far from the horrific scenes described by Grandma and the stench of blood and ashes. I dream of the next football match with the village boys. Marble games. Cartwheels and coconut juice. Mum detaches Nojum from her breast. My sister whines her disapproval. I shudder one last time before sinking into a deep sleep.

3

The highlanders

Mylmin, a village somewhere between
Chin State and Arakan State, 1986

I grab a steaming cup of tea, gulp it down, and am about to dash out of the door of our bamboo hut when my mother's firm hand stops me in my tracks.

'Hey, you rascal, haven't you forgotten something? Stay there a minute, while I make you look handsome!'

Mum sits on a little log and squeezes me between her knees. With gentle fingers, she applies a thick layer of thanaka paste to my arms and face. The subtle scent of the damp bark reminds me of citrus fruit and sandalwood. Mum traces a flawless yellow circle on my smooth cheeks with a toothbrush and draws a perfect line down the bridge of my nose. Nojum stands half-naked on the willow mat in front of us, closely watching proceedings with her big almond eyes. The yellow paste on her face is already dry and a pretty leaf pattern is set into her prominent cheekbones. I pull a face at her. She utters a playful shriek, bursts out laughing, loses her balance, and topples over. Mum puts on a stern look, but her eyes are smiling. She pushes me back to check her handiwork.

'There you go, sweetheart. Your face won't get sunburnt and it'll keep you cool all day long.'

She nuzzles me between my hairline and ear. My head twists back onto my shoulder as I feel her warm lips tickle my skin. She watches me in silence, her eyes shining, her head full of mysterious thoughts. She runs her fingers through my hair and strokes the nape of my neck.

I love her.

'Feed the hens before you go to school. Off you go, scram!' she instructs me.

The sun has barely risen above the valley and our cockerel is crowing at the top of his voice. Dad has already left the hut to go and open his shop. He sells all sorts of things, especially medicines from China and India, and medicinal herbs. He acts as village nurse and administers injections to the sick. He sometimes stays in his shop at night, macerating branches and leaves from Chinese mugwort, a plant used to treat the malaria outbreaks that are common in our region. He also has a herb-and-root-based remedy that has saved me from malaria on several occasions.

As for Grandma, she's always around somewhere. Since she's been living with us, she has added household tasks to the homework that we have to do for school. We milk the goats, gather wood, and make sure that the pitchers of water are always full.

Mum goes to the corner of the room to say her prayers. She rocks her upper body back and forth, tipping her forehead to the ground. I shake Babuli, who wakes up and follows me and Nojum to the chicken coop. We fling seeds to the starving hens. Grandma is already climbing the slope back up from the river, weighed down by two heavy water-buckets hanging either side of a wooden pole balanced on her shoulders. In my cloth bag, the little parcel of fried rice that Mum has prepared for my lunch bangs against my leg as I walk. Babuli, Nojum, and I make our way to the school, a simple wooden shack with a big blackboard on which we learn how to read, write, and count.

The word 'Rohingya' is forbidden. We only use it among ourselves in the hut. It is our secret identity. Dad insists that we use the term 'Muslim' when we introduce ourselves. If we say that we are Rohingya, we would be signing the family's death warrant, he says. So we never do.

For me and Babuli, the word 'Rohingya' evokes hidden danger but also immense pride. It is a connection that brings us closer to cousins, uncles, aunts, and friends who we have never met, who live in Arakan, the neighbouring region. Most of our people are concentrated there. Dad explained to us that if we ever had to flee our home, there would always be someone somewhere who would help us — just whisper the password 'Rohingya'. Babuli and I don't yet understand the gravity of the situation; we sometimes mischievously say this forbidden word in secret to one another when Dad isn't around.

Our village sits on the shores of the Kaladan River and is surrounded by wooded mountains that mark the boundary between Arakan State and Chin State. It is a multicultural crossroads. The villagers are descended from many different ethnic groups, speak many different languages, and include Christians, animists, Muslims, and Buddhists. The animist Khumis form the majority, followed by a large number of Christian Matus and Zomis, some Buddhist Bamars and

Rakhines, who are closely associated with the governing powers, and twenty or so Muslim families, in other words us, the Rohingya. But we keep that quiet!

My Khumi friends call me 'the Muslim' to differentiate between me and the rest of the group, but it is always said in an affectionate, teasing way. However, the children from the Buddhist Bamar and Rakhine ethnic groups refuse to call me and my family anything other than *kalars*, said in a spiteful and aggressive tone. I hate it when they shout this name, as if they were spitting into our faces. I do my best to ignore them. At home, we speak Arakanese, the language of the region where our family comes from, and at school our lessons are in Burmese. It wasn't until Grandma arrived that I learnt to converse in the Rohingya dialect, which she often uses to speak privately with Dad. A few months ago, my parents decided that it was time for me to learn the family language. So at weekends, I attend a clandestine class for Rohingya given by Mr Hafiz, a skinny old man with a neat white beard and an affable manner.

In the village, everyone knows everyone else, relationships are genuine, and people are good-natured. They are mountain dwellers, hunters and gatherers, farmers and fishermen. I love wandering around the market with my best friends, Froo Win, Phyo, and Tutu, looking at the vegetables, mushrooms, fresh herbs, plants, and small game brought by neighbouring tribes. The market traders arrange their produce on wooden boards and stalls or in small willow baskets set on the ground. Each is hoping to make a few coins from the fruits of their backbreaking work in the extremely fertile — but hostile — environments of the forests and steep, rocky hills. When I hear the foghorn, I rush down the road to the jetty just as the barges laden with fruit and vegetables arrive from other regions. Everyone is jostling to get a good deal; bids ring out from all sides as produce is traded. My friends and I enjoy speculating and placing bets on whether Mrs Khin, the stocky-waisted Zomi woman with a blue comb in her bun, or Mr Boba, the old Khumi warrior, will bag the big fish on the stall, and at what price. Another of our games is guessing the price of produce before anyone else.

In class, Mr Milyor, our teacher, a considerate and accommodating Christian, makes us sit on the ground to sing the national anthem:

> *Until the world fragments, long live Burma!*
> *We love our land because it is our true inheritance.*
> *We will sacrifice our lives to protect our nation.*
> *This is our country, this is our land, and it belongs to us.*
> *We will come together and unite for our nation and our land.*
> *This is our duty towards our precious land.*

The rest of the day is spent repeating lessons in chorus. English is one of my favourite subjects; it is an easy language to learn, whereas the rest of our lessons — given in Burmese, with its alphabet of thirty-three letters and twenty phonetic symbols — are really difficult. The teacher makes us mix and read together. Thanks to him, I make friends with Christian and animist children who I don't normally see in my neighbourhood. That's how I met my gang of pals.

On the way back from school, Froo Win, Tutu, Phyo, and I make a beeline for the river where we'll splash around and do acrobatics in the water. The thought of the cold water gives us wings.

As we are walking along the track to the little hillock that we use as a diving board, we pass a group of young Rakhines the same age as us, squatting on the ground playing hopscotch. They break off their game as we go by. Three of them hurl abuse at me:

'Look who it is! Look at the dirty *kalar* who believes in his *kalar* God! Is he on his way to wash off his filth?'

'With his big nose, big eyebrows, and big ears, he's more hideous than an ogre.'

'Forget the thanaka, nigger. You can't hide your pongy *kalar* skin.'

The usual stuff.

The Rakhines have got it in for me. There aren't many of them, but their hatred and aggression give them a self-assurance that sends shivers down my spine. Then, the first stone hits me. Others are already being aimed. I turn towards them to try to dodge the next ones. Dad has told me to never react physically. Only words can bring justice.

'*Kalar* yourself!' I shout. 'Your God is a *kalar* too and your nose is bigger than mine for starters. Look at it spread all over your cheeks. Watch out, you won't be able to breathe soon!'

I'm quite proud of my retort. I give my friends a knowing look. Our adversaries are boiling with rage.

'Get lost, you pighead! You stink of dung! Poo!'

'Why don't you get rid of all that dung up your nose? It'll be better then, you'll see.'

My friends and I hurry on. Behind us, the group refuse to let up; they start singing as they carry on throwing stones at me: '*The* kalar *eats peas, he slips under the pea tree and — thud! splat! — the* kalar *is dead. It's the month of* Waso† *and* kalarma *dance and dance in circles round him.*'

---

† A Buddhist festival similar to Lent. For three months, Buddhist monks retreat into monasteries to meditate. During this period, donations to monks increase.

I clap my hands over my ears and start shouting to block out their stupid remarks: 'Rakhine, Rakhine, sit on your bamboo chair like a lazy slob. Oh no, you can't, it pinches your goolies. Ouch! Hahaha!'

We burst out laughing and take off at speed. We are highlanders, mountain people. No one can run faster than us. Once we reach the river, I whip off my *longyi* and leap from the top of the mound of earth. I spring into the air, toes pointed skywards, and dive into the water. Froo Win, with his stocky, awkward body, almost collides with me.

Day fades and the sky turns orange, transforming the river into a wonderful mirror of golden reflections.

'It'll be dark soon! Quick!'

I climb out of the water, get dressed, and run through the village to our hut. I sneak in noiselessly behind Grandma's *longyi*. I recognise the smell of perfumed rice.

'What have you been up to now, you scoundrel? Wipe your face with this damp cloth.'

Dad comes in behind me carrying some logs that he puts down in the corner. He seizes my jaw, forcing me to look him straight in the eye. He is furious.

'Where have you been? Look, it's already dark. I've told you that it's dangerous to come back late. Don't go too far from the house. You could be arrested by soldiers or police, or stopped by nasty Rakhines, and we wouldn't be able to do a thing to help you. Do you understand?'

His hand leaves a mark on my cheek. I steel myself in anticipation of what's to come. Tears well up in my eyes. A slap stings the other cheek. I take the blows and feel my heart clench at the idea that I have disappointed him.

'You are a Rohingya, Habib. You must not play with just

anybody, anywhere and anyhow. You must know your place. You have to be more responsible than children from other ethnic groups. You are not like them. Play is a luxury that we cannot allow ourselves. You would do better to study or help us.'

I look down, arms hanging stiffly at my sides, contrite. Mum walks past the door, carrying earthenware jars of water that she pours into a cooking pot.

'Come and sit here now.' Dad beckons me onto his lap and picks up a long stick. His demeanour has changed, as if he has already forgiven me. I throw myself into his arms and settle on his muscular thighs.

'Watch carefully and memorise every single one of my gestures. I want you to be as educated as possible. It's for your own good. It will save your life sooner than you think.'

Dad draws some shapes on the ground and explains geometry to me. It won't be long before I'll know everything I need to know. Week after week, Dad gives me extracurricular lessons. I will soon be ahead of the other children in my class.

Despite his warnings and my heavy homework schedule, he sometimes lets me play with Babuli and my sisters Rohima and Nojum. We play hide-and-seek, chess, riddles, charades, bamboo-leaf blowing, ball games, and *pyit taing htaung*†, and we're sometimes allowed to splash about in the water. But these moments of fun are increasingly rare.

One evening, I watch through the window as my brother and sisters tease our two puppies in the courtyard in front of the house. I start daydreaming that I'm out there with them, flapping big palm leaves and making the little dogs jump.

---

† A traditional Burmese toy made from teak. *Pyit taing htaung* literally means 'always rights itself when thrown to the ground', in reference to the spherical shape of the toy, which rolls back up when pushed. The game is known as Myanmar Tumbling Kelly in English.

Suddenly a rattan stick is slammed down on my hands. Dad has spotted my attention drifting and throws me a black look.

'Do you want to live in servitude? Do you want to slave away, and take the place of oxen in front of carts transporting rice that you'll be taxed more for than the others? If that's what you want, go outside and play!'

I'm ashamed.

'No, Dad.'

'Then don't just do what someone asks of you. Do more! It's not just a question of knowledge, Habib, it's a question of survival. If you want to be a grown-up, you'll have to stop constantly thinking about playing. You have to study if you want to avoid the fate that the Burmese regime has chosen for us. Education is the key to emancipation.'

Dad waves his stick around and draws shapes in the beaten earth of the hut.

'What's that?'

'An equilateral triangle, Dad.'

'Well done. Now, draw me a square.'

We carry on with the lesson until he decides that it is my bedtime. I choose the moment to ask him a question that has been bothering me since the altercation with the Rakhines.

'Dad, what's the difference between gods? Is there such a thing as a *kalar* god?'

'All men have the same God, Habib. But we have different beliefs and an image of God that is specific to us. From all these different interpretations, we get what we call religions, and the thing that guarantees peaceful coexistence between these religions is tolerance. Only idiots use the word *kalar*. Don't listen to them. You haven't got time to waste on them. Off you go and say your prayers with Mum.'

I run off to join my mother. I do my ablutions, unfold the little prayer mat that she has woven for me, and squat down under her watchful eye.

'Habib, one thing you can do when you pray is to thank God for what you have and for the courage that He continues to give you. No need to make it too long or complicated. Prayer is a way of showing that you are present and expressing your gratitude.'

As I bow, I imagine that God has granted me superpowers so that I can provide my family with plenty of fish and curry every day. I gradually let myself go and my head droops. A little tap on the shoulder pulls me back into line.

'You don't fall asleep in front of God!'

When it comes to religion, Grandma is always there to keep a beady eye on proceedings.

'It's bedtime, you rascal. One last bow and off to bed with you, my little one.'

4

'Mum, don't leave me'

'I'm not leaving you, Habib. I'm taking you with me in my heart — you, your brother, and your sisters. I'll always be here, Habib. Here, in this special place of love.'

Mum gently traces a little circle on my chest. She carries on whispering into my ear, her warm palm on my cheek.

'At night, when it's dark, think of the moon and the stars. They are the light of hope, our eternal guardians. Wherever you are and wherever I am, they will bring you the messages that I'll send.'

She inhales deeply into my neck to take a bit of my smell with her. I grab a fistful of her *longyi* and cling on hard to stop her from leaving, as I beg her: 'Mum, please don't go. Please don't leave us.'

'There's nothing I can do about it, Habib. Pay attention to what Dad, Auntie Kulama, and Auntie Fuma tell you. They are going to look after you. Mummy has to go. I don't have any choice, believe me. We can't always do what we want. Promise me that you'll be good, that you'll work hard at school and help your dad. You're the oldest, so set a good example for your brother and sisters. I'm relying on you, darling.'

She is leaving. But I don't know where, why, or for how long. I don't understand. I'm bewildered.

'Mum, are you going to come back?'

Her eyes are shining. She doesn't answer. My vision blurs over. Tears stream down my cheeks. My throat is taut with grief. Why is Mum going? Why is she leaving us? Have I been disobedient? Where is she going?

Dad carries her bags to the jetty. As usual, before anyone from our family is allowed to board a boat, we are taken to one side. The authorities subject us to special treatment because we are Rohingya. They are speaking to my parents and searching all their bundles. Dad gives them a wad of notes. They ask for more. It's the *kalar* tax. Mum finally takes her place with the others on the boat. She stares at me with trembling lips and a melancholic smile. I watch as she gradually vanishes into the mist suspended above the river. My sisters are crying in my aunts' arms. Babuli and I both panic, and we run along beside the boat as it departs and clamber up onto the highest part of the riverbank. I recognise her silhouette and see that she has managed to squeeze into a tiny spot among the passengers at the front. Then suddenly she disappears behind the rice fields.

Dad stands there for a long time in silence before turning on his heels and striding up the mud track. I realise that he doesn't want any of us to follow him.

'Come on, Habib, I'll buy you a tamarind sweet.'

Auntie Kulama tries to distract me. I look at her, bewildered and dazed, then turn to stare again at the horizon over which my mother has vanished. This can't be real. She can't have gone. I'm hoping that the boat will turn around, and that Mum will come back and give me a reassuring hug. How am I going to live without her? I feel a light pressure on my wrist, Auntie Fuma is trying to pull me away from the riverbank onto the wooden jetty. I haven't the energy to resist and I let her guide me.

Fuma holds out a plastic football to Babuli and me.

'That's from your mum.'

I dry my tears and wipe my nose on the corner of my shirt. I take the ball, roll it along the ground, and kick it half-heartedly to Babuli, who passes it back to me without enthusiasm. When we get home, the hut seems empty.

That evening, beneath the big tamarind tree next to the hut, my aunts cradle all four of us in silence as we look out at the uninterrupted view of the valley, the river, and the mountains. The moon seems brighter to me, despite the dark clouds that threaten to obscure it. I am convinced that Mum is also staring at the bright light of the moon at this very moment. I close my eyes to imagine her face as I snuggle up to Fuma, who starts singing a nursery rhyme:

'If the rain falls, then you'll be drenched, drenched, drenched. If your Mummy comes ... If your Daddy comes ... Then you'll eat coconuts, nuts, nuts.'

I start humming along with her.

'The rain will fall ... Mummy will come ... We'll eat coconuts.'

Lying in my auntie's arms as she gently strokes my hair, I forget everything. She carries on singing:

'Read my letter, Fyu Fyu ... I'd give my life for you ... That's how much I love you ... Fyu Fyu ... Take it, take it ... If you have faith in me, then take it ...'

I suddenly hear Mum's words: 'At night, when it's dark, think of the moon and the stars. They are the light of hope, our eternal guardians. Wherever you are and wherever I am, they will bring you the messages that I'll send.'

To this day, I still don't know why my mother went on that journey. Nor what happened when she arrived in the unknown place that I've only ever seen in my dreams.

5

Nature's school

Froo Win, my best friend, leaps from rocks to mossy clumps of earth like a hare. He helps his parents bring in the harvest from the fields and forage for food in the mountains, and is stronger and more agile than anyone I know. I make fun of him for his round pink and yellow face, while he never misses an opportunity to remark on my dark, bushy eyebrows. Between ourselves, this kind of teasing is acceptable.

Although Froo Win is not a Rohingya — he has Rakhine and Khumi ancestors — we are drawn to one another. We both have vivid imaginations and believe that we belong to the same tribe of proud 'highlanders'. We are barely eight years old, but we are already emperors of our world.

I challenge him to a race; we weave in and out of the bushes and play at trying to scare one another. Laughing and carefree, we zig-zag between the trees, using the tall ferns as camouflage. When we are too breathless to run any more, we stop and scrutinise the horizon to see which trees in the forest are groaning with fruit. We climb the broad trunks of the teak and banyan trees that have hollows at the top where we can sit devouring our spoils, and share stories and dreams. Then the tickling matches and the games of hide-and-seek and tag resume.

We are the kings of the forest. I have the power to fly. He has the power of invisibility. He leaps into the air; I climb onto huge rocks. We soar like eagles to the top of the mountain, where the waterfall drops over the edge. First, we are birds high in the mountains; then, we are fish in the river, or big cats in the wild. We are intoxicated by nature.

Some odd-looking sticks decorated with leaves and balls of wild cotton have been planted in the stream by villagers from Froo Win's tribe. My friend signals to me to stop.

'Look Habib, the mountain spirits are conferring.'

Froo Win, who is both Christian and animist, explains to me that the mountain spirits instructed the shaman of his tribe to erect this temporary altar.

I throw him a bemused, questioning look. He continues with his explanation.

'Once the spirits have finished their meeting, the river will carry the sticks away, and the spirits will fly off in different directions across many lands to protect our people.'

He tells me that his grandparents frequently call on the spirits to protect their house and family. They never make decisions without consulting the gods, whereas his parents worship the Christian God. Froo Win's grandfather has always lived in Mylmin, our village. He has an amazing collection of bows and arrows. He is a better archer than anyone and can bring down any forest animal. One day he taught us how to use catapults to catch birds on the wing.

I never knew my own grandfather, who used to live with my grandmother and father in nearby Arakan State, before our family were chased away by men from the dominant tribe, the Rakhines. Or maybe it was the Burmese soldiers. I can't remember anymore. Whichever it was, my grandfather was arrested and tortured to death. Grandma often cries when she talks about him. The rest of the family went into hiding while they waited for the manhunt to end.

I sit down next to the waterfall and open a leaf in which Auntie Fuma has wrapped citronella-flavoured rice. Froo Win's mother has made him a salad of acacia leaves and turmeric flowers with a big naan bread. In the distance, we can hear the village children congregating on the football pitch. I recognise the voices of Nai and Kyaw, two friends who love the beautiful game as much as I do, and we jump up and hurry off to join them. Football is my passion, but I am not allowed to enter school or village competitions because I am Muslim and black. Nonetheless, my teachers, who are from the minority Chin group, let me join in some of the training sessions like this one. During these sessions, nothing else matters. All I think of is the game, the strategy, and the adrenaline of winning.

These moments united us through a shared language that ignored skin colour, religion, and origins: the universal language of sport.

On the way home, I am scared of what Dad will say. I have been out all day and he'll scold me like he always does every time I stay too long in the mountains, the only place where I can be free.

6

The frontier of happiness

1988

'*Ne Win, son of a whore!*'
  '*Light of glory, light of despair!*'
  '*Police beggars, soldier thieves!*'
  '*Sein Lwin†, king of murderers!*'
The villagers march through the streets of Mylmin, brandishing multi-coloured banners and chanting at the tops of their voices. The entire village — from local government workers to students and farmers — is out demonstrating, confident that Ne Win's dictatorship can now finally be overturned, after years of repression and terror.

Tutu, Phyo, Froo Win, Kyaw, and I are overexcited, elated by this new wind of freedom. At the back of the crowd, we mimic the adults and raise our fists, before dashing to the front of

---

† Sein Lwin, Burmese soldier and politician, Ne Win's right-hand man, was briefly president of Burma during the pro-democratic uprising of 1988.

the procession, exclaiming: 'Watch out, Ne Win! We are the highlanders and we're coming to get you!'

But play soon takes precedence over our urge to protest. In the middle of the demonstration, we start up a game of tag. We split up and weave our way in and out of the marchers.

Villagers of all colours, religions, and ethnic groups are marching arm in arm. Rohingya, Khumis, Bamars, Rahkines, all together with the same voice and the same determination. 'Highlanders!' 'Freedom!'

A few days later, gunshots echo a chilling warning across the village. Soldiers have emerged from the forests, the river, and the surrounding plains, and taken up residence *en masse*. They lay siege to our little world deep in the mountains. Multiple arrests are made. People are screaming and crying. For the first time, I witness neighbours, men and women alike, being dragged away from their families and taken I don't know where. I never see them again. The days go by and a hush descends over the village. The procession is over. Expressions harden. No more singing, no more protesting. The village is plunged into absolute silence. Soldiers patrol around the houses, sowing terror wherever they go. Spies skulk everywhere, and suspicion grows. The solidarity that united us is shattered, replaced by fear.

At home, Dad is sick with worry. He has been removed from his post at the workers' association. My aunts try to keep calm by concentrating on the housework. Their usual cheerfulness has vanished, and their silence unsettles me and my brother and sisters.

My Uncle Dim, who lives in another village, is due to arrive today. He is a larger-than-life character, always full of joy, who never misses an opportunity to crack a joke and make us laugh.

I have wonderful memories of his last visit, several years ago. My parents often talk about him. His presence will surely bring some good humour to the household. I am excited just at the idea of giving him a hug. I am so looking forward to his arrival that I bombard my aunts with questions about him.

When my father reappears alone in the doorway of our hut, looking distraught, my enthusiasm evaporates. Dad walks over to the table, where he starts gathering together important documents. Auntie Kulama rushes to his side.

'What's happened?'

Dad stops leafing through his papers and turns to her with a serious look.

'He was arrested by the authorities as soon as he set foot on the jetty. The same old story: breaking the law that forbids Muslims to travel outside their village. They've taken him away. We have to act quickly.'

Auntie Kulama and Auntie Fuma glance at one another and the blood drains from their faces. Auntie Fuma stumbles and catches herself on one of the bamboo walls of the hut. She struggles to contain the tears that she hurriedly wipes away with the back of her hand. Auntie Kulama helps her to sit down.

Dad eventually manages to find what he is looking for — an envelope hidden inside a bamboo cane. He removes a thick bundle of banknotes.

'I'm going back to the police station. As long as he hasn't been sent to the military camp, there's still time for me to negotiate his freedom.'

Before he leaves, Dad lifts me up onto his lap. Since I turned ten, he has taken to speaking to me like this, man to man.

'Habib, there are some things that you will understand later, but for now you must listen to me. You are a Rohingya, never forget that, but you must never again say this word when you are with people from other ethnic groups, even your best friend.'

He squeezes my arm and shakes it until I look at him right in the eye.

'Never. Do you understand?'

'Yes, Dad.'

'You can say that you are a Muslim. But if you say that you are Rohingya, they will lock you away and then kill you. We all have to stick together even if it costs us the last kyat[†] of our savings. The authorities want one of two things: to eliminate us or to strip us bare. Our blood or our money. Policing in Burma is corrupt to the core, but it's also thanks to this corruption that we can buy our freedom. Think about it.'

The next day, Dad returns from the police station, supporting Uncle Dim, who is shuffling. When he sees me, he manages a tiny glimmer of a smile and pinches my cheek. After swallowing some tea and eating a plate of rice with chilli sauce, he tries to lie down, helped by Auntie Fuma, who is attentive to his every need. He has been beaten on his stomach and the back of his neck, and is in such pain that no position is comfortable for him. His swollen eyelids disfigure his face.

Ever since the demonstrations, school has been closed. My uncle's arrival reminds me of Grandma, who returned to her village a few months ago. I miss her presence and even her long stories.

Now that we are on enforced holiday, I ask my father, 'Dad, can we go and see Grandma?'

'No Habib, we're not allowed to leave the village.'

'But why are my friends allowed to leave?'

---

† Burmese currency.

'Your friends are not Muslims, Habib.'

'Will we ever be able to leave?'

'We'll try to bribe the authorities so that Grandma can come and see us. I promise, son.'

I spend a dismal evening trying to untangle my confused thoughts and questions: *Why am I not treated the same as my friends? Why am I the only one to be confined within the perimeter of our village? Why was my uncle beaten?* A sense of injustice gnaws away at me.

The following day, I play with my brother and sisters in the yard as if everything were normal again. As it turns out, I barely have time to enjoy being off school before Dad decides that he'll personally take over from my teacher while we wait for classes to begin again. So, every morning at dawn, my brother and I go with him to his shop, where he now sells a wider range of products including shirts and *longyis*, fabrics, bags, and groceries, while continuing to offer medical treatment to the villagers, who come to him for daily consultations and trust him implicitly. He prepares traditional concoctions from Burma, China, India, and the West.

For me, it is the start of a new school of life. It is around this time that Dad gives me my first book: an encyclopaedia of medicinal herbs. He also teaches me about business and the art of negotiation and, more importantly, the art of listening — paying particular attention to people's aches and pains; observing, investigating, and understanding. With each sick person who comes to see him, Dad takes time to interpret their symptoms and what brought them on. He treats malaria, flu, bronchitis, migraines, wounds, and diarrhoea caused by filthy water. He teaches me to give injections, and about the properties of plants, such as cardamom for relieving gas and stomach pain. Dad can cure anything, except for illnesses that require surgery.

This morning, like all the others, I wake up, hair tousled. I pull on my *longyi* and T-shirt and shake Babuli awake.

'Come on, time to get up, lazy bones.'

Babuli mutters and sits up mechanically, still half asleep, eyes half closed. A swift prayer, a cup of tea, and I am ready to go.

Dad is busy writing a letter and beckons me over.

'Habib, come here. I'm not going to open the shop today. I have to go and talk to the pastor and some other villagers. Listen, what I have to tell you is important. I want you to spend the day thinking about it seriously while I'm out.'

I sit down cross-legged, all ears, looking directly at him. He comes up to me and wraps his arms around my shoulders.

'Before I fled the village in Arakan where I was born, I was a leader who was respected by the Rohingya, but also by members of other ethnic groups. The secret is tolerance and accepting differences. You have to be open to the people around you without imposing your beliefs or your choices on them, and you need to know how to listen and find grounds for understanding, which is how people are able to live together.'

His arms gently tighten their grip on my shoulders. He continues: 'Your actions will define you, much more so than your prayers. Ignorance and certainty only generate hatred. Instead, learning from others, analysing, confronting, and questioning things make you more open to the world. Even if you have obligations of your own, it's good to give some time to those in need, particularly those from other communities. You see, I'm going to take some time today to meet our Christian, animist, and perhaps even Buddhist neighbours.'

He pauses before going on, cupping his hands around my face when he sees my attention drifting: 'So, tell me what is most important.'

'Tolerance, Dad.'

'Exactly. Right, work hard today and don't forget to go and fill up the buckets with water. We've nearly run out.'

Once he's gone, I leaf through the pages of the botany book. I'm fascinated by the pictures and words that explain the properties of each plant. Then I see Froo Win walking past my house.

'Hi! Aren't you working today?'

'No, my dad has things to do. What are you doing?'

'I'm going to hunt birds with a catapult. Do you want to come with me?'

'Dad has forbidden me to leave the neighbourhood.'

'We won't tell him then! If we go through the bushes, no one will see you.'

'Okay.'

'Let's meet in my backyard. I'm going to find the others!'

My friends — Froo Win; Tutu, an animist Khumi; Phyo, a Buddhist Khumi; and Kyaw, a Christian Chin — are all different. Although we don't have the same backgrounds, this doesn't stop us being friends. We sneak behind Froo Win's hut and up the hillside towards the forest. The day goes quickly; we catch two big fish in the river and climb up the mountainside where lots of birds live. With the catapult that belongs to Froo Win's grandfather, we take aim at parrots, tits, and horn bills, which dodge our stones with impressive dexterity. Froo Win eventually manages to bring down a spotted ground thrush that he kills and puts in his willow basket as a trophy.

'Halt!'

A gunshot stops us in our tracks.

'You there, halt!'

A battalion of around 30 menacing soldiers in helmets stands in front of us pointing weapons in our direction. We are petrified. My throat seizes up and I think of Dad.

The captain bellows at the top of his lungs: 'Who are you? What are you doing here?'

Froo Win takes his courage in both hands and says in a trembling voice: 'We are children from the village. We were only playing.'

'You're not supposed to be in these mountains. It's a black zone. Do you know what a black zone is, you imbecile?'

'Sorry sir. We won't do it again.'

'Clear off immediately. Get out of here!'

'Yes sir.'

The soldiers watch us for a minute before vanishing themselves.

We rush headlong down the hill towards the village and, once we are out of earshot of the soldiers, Froo Win turns to us and shouts in a booming voice: 'Who goes there? Stop, you filthy bandits!'

I carry on the game by brandishing a stick at my friends. 'You're in the black zone. You must be killed! Bang, bang!'

Tay Tan pretends to fall down dead, while Tun Tin and Froo Win drop to the ground and point their weapons at me.

We chase one another down the mountain and this helps us to forget our bad experience.

The approach of dusk reminds us that it is time to go home. Dad has been waiting for me for ages. I walk towards him awkwardly, embarrassed. He knows where I've been, but says nothing, just pushes me against the bamboo wall. He gives me two lashes on the back with a stick. He grits his teeth in an attempt to stifle his cries of rage so that the neighbours won't hear him.

'I told you not to go into the mountains anymore without me. The black zone is forbidden to Muslims. You're putting your life in danger.'

Later, lying in bed, I think about what he said. The black zone, the soldiers who aimed their weapons at us. Perhaps the presence of my Christian and animist friends saved my life today.

7

Buddha's tax

I proudly hand over the change to a teenage Khumi boy who has just bought some of my aunt's homemade fritters. I am 11 now and old enough to deputise for Dad in his shop. He trusts me enough that he can take a back seat and concentrate on his patients. In the rear of the shop, a desperate-looking farmer sits on a small wooden chair as Dad palpates his veins and listens to his heartbeat. He is saying to my father in a bitter tone: 'This brain virus that makes the cows go mad has killed a hundred animals in the village and it seems to be attacking humans now. It's a catastrophe. How will we survive such a plague? I would have got a good price for the two oxen I had. We could have lived on that for a few months. God knows we need the money at the moment.'

The army is patrolling near the market, on the lookout for any slight transgression that might give them an excuse to punish someone. Anyone who crosses their path had better watch out. As usual, the soldiers also come looking for gifts and money, preferably from Muslim business-owners. They impose an extra tax on us because we *kalars* are the 'invaders'. They are particularly fond of Dad's shop. I see one of them walking towards us. He nonchalantly enters the shop in a way intended to provoke. He runs his fingers along some of the merchandise on the shelves and examines the medicines before looking my father up and down with a sardonic laugh, daring him to react.

'So, *kalar*, business is good it seems.'

He grabs a packet of biscuits and a few sachets of sweet white coffee mix. The farmer makes himself scarce, surreptitiously leaving a few notes on a shelf, out of the soldier's sight. Dad stands up and pushes me behind him, pressing my forehead into his hip. He stares impassively at the soldier, showing no sign of bitterness, hatred, rancour, rebellion, or submission, no visible emotion. He has told me that you must remain neutral when the army takes a dislike to you, and adopts this attitude each week when the soldiers come here to extort money and goods from us. The soldier fills both his pockets with booty. He belches loudly, spits on the ground, and departs just as he arrived. The red spittle from the juice of the betel nut that he was chewing leaves a bitter stain. I swiftly throw a small bucket of water on it to erase the bad memory.

Dad remains silent. Lips pursed, he tidies the shelf before pulling me onto his lap and giving me a long hug during which I sense just how powerless and disconcerted he feels. Without saying a word about what has just happened, he eventually gets a grip on himself. He pours me a cup of tea, and writes a difficult maths equation for me to solve. I work on it while he goes into the backyard to be alone.

Some time later, Captain KZW, a cruel man from Rakhine who relishes his job as head of law and order in our area, announces that every villager will be required to help build a pagoda for worshipping Buddha. One member of each family will be requisitioned every day to participate in the construction work. The pagoda will be erected on the mountaintop at the exact spot where Christians have been gathering, holding sermons, and celebrating religious festivals, including Christmas, for generations. As minority groups, we all feel affected by this decision, which is a sure sign of worse to come. Each family has to make a 'voluntary' donation of a thousand kyats, the equivalent of several days' income for most households. There is no question of not paying. Those who are unable to raise the sum required will be sent to prison.

David, one of Dad's Christian patients, and leader of the Khumi neighbourhood, can barely contain his outrage. As my father administers him a fever vaccine, he exclaims, 'Why is the army meddling with religious matters in the village? Why are the Buddhist authorities allowing such abuses to be committed in their name? Destroying our place of worship to replace it with theirs is totally unacceptable! There are vast forests around here, so many places where they could have built this pagoda. What is all this supposed to mean? That they want to make the country Buddhist and trample all other religions underfoot? Doesn't making Christians, Muslims, Hindus, and animists pay for their religion go against their principles?'

'They don't need the soldiers. If the monks want our help to build their temples, they just need to ask us. They don't need to go through the army. I would be happy to help if they weren't forcing us,' Dad comments.

From now on, all the land around the village is declared

a black zone, forbidden to Muslims. My family is not allowed to enter the jungle under any circumstances, whether to collect wood or visit a neighbouring village. Dad tells us that we can only play behind our home. However, he still needs to restock his shop regularly and has no choice but to enter the jungle in secret to gather plants or reach supply points in surrounding villages.

One day, we are told that the soldiers have left to search for Chin rebels in the mountains. My father and I seize the opportunity to enter the forbidden zones. We gather leaves and wood to make brooms that Dad will sell. Equipped with knives, ropes and catapults, and some rice, dried fish, and chilli to eat, we move quickly and stealthily through the trees. My father keeps a lookout for any danger, and I copy him. Every branch that snaps makes us jump. We return home before sunset with armfuls of twigs and long sticks.

The sun's orange-red orb slowly dips below the hills of Chin State. From our house on the high ground, I watch the military camp by the river. One of the military intelligence units, known as MI-10, is stationed there. In the enclosed yard, the soldiers are making prisoners in leg irons do squats and sit-ups while beating them incessantly with apparent sadistic pleasure. A shiver runs down my spine.

8

Minor escapades

Dad has gone to no end of trouble to enrol me in secondary school. He has a dream that would be impossible in anyone else's eyes and that no one but us knows about: he wants his children to become lawyers.

My new school is an old two-storey building, a vestige of the British colonial period, and is attended by children from the remote mountain villages. Lessons began a month ago. There are only a dozen Rohingya, spread across different classes and subjects. The other pupils number almost a thousand from diverse ethnic groups, with a majority of Chins, Khumis, and Rakhines. We all have our own dialects, but at school we have to speak Burmese. By now, I speak three languages fluently — Rakhine at home, Burmese at school, and Rohingya at the religious school that I continue to attend at weekends.

I have endless admiration, appreciation, and love for my teachers. The government pays them a pittance that barely covers the cost of their uniforms. Most of their income comes from the fishing and farm work that they do in their free time. Whenever any of the parents bump into the teachers at the market, they are always effusive in their praise and gratitude for these extraordinary, knowledgeable, and passionate men and women who are devoted to their community. I often see one of my favourite teachers, Saya Naing, outside school in his small canoe laden with herbs and fish. He is a humble, hard-working man who makes a point of not differentiating me from the other pupils despite the constant bullying by young Rakhines my age. He treats everyone as equals.

At the start of the school day, we file into the classroom and squeeze in side by side on the wooden benches behind long narrow desks. There is one book for every four pupils. The majority of children in my class are poor, and not everyone can afford the compulsory uniform, but the headmaster is not strict about that.

The bell rings, and we run outside for lunch. Groups form. I am hurrying out of the building to join Froo Win, Thura, and Tun Tin when my foot hits something that sends me flying head-first to the ground. Someone has tripped me up. Four Rakhine teenagers burst out laughing behind me.

'So, *kalar*, can't stay on your feet then?'

'Your big eyebrows stop you from seeing where you're going, do they?'

They wander off, laughing.

Thura and Tun Tin rush over to help me up.

Incidents like this are part of my daily lot.

Froo Win has been disappearing more and more frequently these past few weeks. I don't see him at school much anymore. One afternoon after class, a huge smile lights up his mischievous round face as he asks me: 'Have you ever seen an action film?'

The truth is, I've never really seen any films, just the old movie posters outside the little village shop where they screen videos.

'Want to come with me to see one?'

I hesitate, torn between desire and guilt.

'What about our lessons?'

'If we don't go this afternoon, our parents won't let us go in the evening, that's for sure.'

Without giving it a further thought, I decide that it's now or never. Curiosity gets the better of me. There are so many pupils that Saya Naing won't notice that I'm not there. Froo Win hands a few kyats to the projectionist, who ushers us into the little curtained-off bamboo room that serves as a cinema. We push our way through the spectators sitting cross-legged on the beaten earth floor, already totally absorbed by the images on the screen. It's a Burmese film.

Dancing, danger, betrayal, friendship, love, and amazing actors. I spend an hour with all kinds of different sensations coursing through my body that until now were completely alien to me. I leave the room with my head full of the images and dreams of this other world. We are both totally over-excited and re-enact different scenes from the film, complete with exaggerated gestures and lengthy speeches, imitating the actress's entreaties and the wounded honour of the jealous man. We walk along the riverbank, reliving the film, until other pupils join us and we know that classes are over for the day.

I race home. Dad has clearly been waiting for me.

'Your teacher Saya Naing has just come by to see if you were sick. Where were you?'

I'm speechless and stare guiltily at the ground. I haven't prepared any excuse.

He pushes me into the backyard and takes his stick.

'Bend over.'

He lashes my back. Once, twice, five times. He is furious. I don't cry out.

When I go into the classroom the next day, the teacher waits for everyone to sit down before calling me up to his desk. The whip awaits, again.

Once again, I take the punishment.

9

The homecoming

'Your mum is back!'

I feel like I'm dreaming. She has been gone for over four years and suddenly she appears in the doorway, arms outstretched and lips trembling just like they did when she left us. I am rooted to the spot for an instant, overcome with emotion; then I throw myself at her, followed by Babuli, Rohima, and Nojum. I pinch her arm just to be sure. It's her, it's Mum! She kneels down and enfolds all four of us in her arms. No one says a word or asks any questions. We are just happy that she is here, with us. She's here. That's all. She's here. Nothing else matters.

'I won't leave you again, my children.'

The reason for her absence is a mystery that will plague me my entire life. It is and always will be a taboo subject. Was she imprisoned, tortured, abused? Like so many Rohingya women, she will never talk about it. My sisters, brother, and I will never ask.

That evening, she's the one who lights the fire, with all the symbolism that entails. The flames crackle as if they are dancing for joy with us. Nojum, Rohima, Babuli, and I sit upright, overwhelmed and a little timid. It has been so long since our mother left. She serves us a bowl of sticky rice prepared as only she knows how. The taste brings back memories. I am already struggling to remember how I managed to live without her. She's back with us, her gentle hands and her soothing smell. I hug her with my eyes closed. I've never been so happy.

Life returns to a certain rhythm and continues as before. Sometimes wonderful, but more and more often troubled by the omnipresent threat of the soldiers.

Mum anxiously shakes me awake. 'Habib, hurry darling. The sun is nearly up. You really mustn't be late. Here, take this water bottle and parcel of rice.'

She hangs a little canvas bag across my chest and gives me some final instructions: 'Make sure you do what they tell you, do you understand? Don't forget that they're keeping a close eye on you!'

Yesterday, the district leader came to requisition a member of the family to work on the maintenance of the military camps and the surrounding fences, paths, and gardens. Today it's my turn. Tomorrow it'll be my brother, then my father. My mother sometimes has to take my youngest sister with her.

I'll be absent from school today and will have to catch up later. These requisitions happen on a weekly — sometimes even daily — basis, depending on the mood of the regimental captain.

Once on site, the soldiers dole out unpleasant tasks, order us around, insult us, and beat us at will.

Very early in the morning, I join the others who have been pressed into forced labour. I have brought my shovel and a rattan basket. Before we leave, our district leader shouts out the usual refrain: 'You are volunteers helping to develop the nation. Give your best for the community.'

They collect us and take us to the SLORC[†] premises.

My first task is to carry willow baskets loaded with gravel and empty them along the path between the military camp and the pagoda. Once I've finished, I join the chain passing red bricks from hand to hand as the sun beats down on us. Then I am sent to the top of the mountain to join another boy my age carrying down heavy bamboo canes. We dump them in the military camp where other villagers are busy building a fence. I'm suffering from the heat, and the only break we are allowed is for lunch. We have just a few minutes to gulp down our portion of rice before returning to work even harder than before.

Further off, the Christians are working on the site of a former church that the captain gave the order to demolish several months ago. They are installing officers' latrines under the steely eye of four soldiers who keep a tight grip on their rifles.

Nightfall brings freedom. I arrive back at our hut, exhausted.

I pray that I am never made a porter. This involves accompanying soldiers into the mountains as they hunt down Chin rebels, and is the job that we fear the most. The porters have to cook, carry the supplies and equipment, and are generally treated as whipping boys. It is the most dangerous assignment, and not everyone comes back alive, especially if they happen to be Rohingya. We are powerless against the soldiers, our only protections prayer and fate.

---

† SLORC (State Law and Order Restoration Council). The name used by the Burmese military for the governing body of Burma after the *coup d'état* of 18 September 1988.

10

The captain's toilets

1990

I'm lying on my stomach on the floor, leafing through an old magazine, trying to find the cartoons. Mum is busy patching up my old *longyi*, with Nojum asleep on her lap. All of a sudden, she cries out in surprise, making me jump. With the sun directly behind them, the village leader and Captain KZW have come up the wooden steps unnoticed and walked into our hut without waiting to be invited. Their military uniforms and muscular torsos are imposing. Mum stands up, tipping Nojum off her lap in her haste, just managing to catch her by the arm. I grab Babuli's shirt and pull him towards me. Rohima is already clinging to me. I hide behind Mum; my brother and sisters copy me.

'*Kalarma*, your husband!'

Mum, bowed over as a sign of respect and submissiveness, pushes me forward.

'Habib, go and get your father. Quickly!'

Without hesitation, I run into the backyard where my father is weaving a rope from rattan.

'Dad, the army captain is here.'

He leaps up and dashes into the house. The captain doesn't stand on ceremony.

'*Kalar*, your house is on land that is required by the state. It will be demolished to build the extra toilets that we need.'

Dad turns pale.

'With all due respect, sir, this is where we live. We purchased this land legally. We received a building permit from the authorities.'

The captain turns on his heels.

'The order has been given. I will not return. You and your family are occupying this land illegally.'

That evening, Dad stays up very late. Sitting cross-legged, he writes, crosses out, and copies out in neat. He fills several pages with drafts before producing a letter that he seems happy with. He inserts it into an envelope, which he seals and places on the corner of his little table. Head in hands, fingers buried in his hair, he stares blankly at the grain of the wood, without uttering a word. I go up to him, partly worried, partly curious.

'Dad, what are you doing?'

He pulls me towards him and looks me straight in the eyes as he says, 'You see, Habib, even if everything is conspiring against us, we must never stop claiming what is rightfully ours. It's the only way — learn to say no to injustice and rise up against it. This letter that I've written is addressed to the federal government and I have made a copy for the village leader so that he will inform the captain. Until the federal government has given their approval, he can't do anything.'

Dad fears reprisals. However, luck seems to be on his side because several days later the captain is sent on a special mission in the mountains, and the project to demolish our house is postponed.

Military activities intensify. New Burmese regiments pour into Chin State. They go from village to village hunting down rebels. The mountains are teeming with soldiers, more terrifying than ever. They dig in around us, ready to pounce. I watch them from the doorway of our hut as they descend on the village. Sometimes men are arrested, beaten, and kidnapped. The soldiers attack porters and villagers at random. The choice of target is completely arbitrary. Violence reigns.

Requisitions become more and more frequent. Dad tries to find new ways of making money, selling or trading everything he can, as well as dispensing advice and treating his patients. Life is extremely dangerous for people like my father who are just trying their best to get by. He has to brave the black zones to stock up on supplies, and hope that he is not reported, because if he is caught in the act he'll have to pay, or face dire consequences. Mum prays that we will be spared.

In early autumn, a hundred soldiers enter the village. Dad instructs us not to go out. It has been over five days since I last left the hut. I am copying out my dictation exercises when three soldiers step through the doorway, ignoring us completely. I clasp the exercise book that Dad gave me tightly to my chest. One of the men rifles through the condiments and bags of rice. He takes a jar, a few dishes, and some vegetables that Mum was about to cook. His companions seize two of our chickens and then stroll out nonchalantly as if they had never even been here. They carry on round the huts, just as other soldiers around the village are doing.

There are dark days ahead, and the forced labour becomes increasingly harsh. The village leader calls on everyone to send a family member to the military camp with a financial contribution. Dad asks Mum to go. He hands her the money, and says: 'Give them that. If I go, I'll just end up causing a scene, I won't be able to stop myself.'

A while later, it happens again. The army needs people to transport its stolen provisions to the next camp. They want one person per family, and we have until sunset to decide who it will be.

My parents are worried.

'Whoever goes will never come back.'

Dad extracts a wad of banknotes hidden under a wooden plank beneath his pillow.

'We'll have to tighten our belts for the next few months, but this money is the only way to save our lives.'

After speaking to the village leader, he whispers to Mum: 'None of us will be sent this time.'

I know that this is just a temporary reprieve and that he is still worried.

The next day, at the crack of dawn, 50 or so villagers carrying supplies and weapons snake their way up the hill ahead of the procession of soldiers. They clear a path through the bushy ground with their machetes. Not all of them will return unharmed from the ten-day journey.

I later find out from those who come back that the porters were used as human shields in the rebel and border zones of Chin State. This is common practice in all of Myanmar's ethnic regions.

11

My kingdom

I gallop along the mud track, with my exercise books and text-books tucked under my arm. We've got exams in three months and I am determined to ace every subject. If I allot seven days per subject and my revision is not disturbed by either my parents or the army, I should be ready by the time the exams start.

I have borrowed a magazine and a superhero comic from my neighbour to read during my breaks. Dad has also given me a copy of *The New Light of Myanmar*, the propaganda paper owned by the Burmese junta, and the only newspaper to which we have access. The foreign press is banned, and the country has no independent publications; all information is subject to censorship. The articles are abhorrent and repetitive. They boast of the army's successes against the rebels and publicise the astronomical sums of money 'donated' to Buddhist monks, mainly for building new pagodas adorned with precious gems. Nevertheless, Dad encourages me to read it, so I do.

I realise that if you read between the lines, it all becomes more interesting and also more terrifying. I am starting to better understand what Dad is always trying to explain to me: the military strategy of imposing Buddhism throughout the country to the detriment of other religions, and the utter contempt for minority ethnic groups, particularly us, the Rohingya, who are considered Bengali immigrants.

Dad has been teaching me how to decipher the newspaper. 'Listen, son, this old rag won't teach you anything about world politics, but it is an excellent way of exercising your critical approach. You're twelve now and old enough to understand, I think. After weapons and religion, the media is the dictatorship's third source of power.'

A long way from my neighbourhood, on the forest's edge, high up, a majestic tamarind tree is my secret hideout. It is a huge, imposing tree with a crown of delicate green leaves, and succulent fruit in the form of big pods with fibrous pulp. I climb up the roots and creepers tangled around the thick trunk. Reaching the top, I slide down and am swallowed up in the hollow of the tree, where the fruit-bearing branches extend. A pair of horn bills, surprised by my arrival, fly away, as if making room for me. No one can see me here, and I can read without being disturbed. There is a gentle breeze, the leaves are rustling, and the birds in the jungle are chirping softly. Nestled in the tree, I am free from curious eyes. I open my books, and the magic of the place takes effect. The words in my history book take me on an exhilarating journey. The hours fly by, and in the end all this reading tires me out. I put Napoleon's battles to one side and pick up my exercise books and pencils. Maths and geometry are like a game to me. I scribble things down, cross them out, ponder, find the answer, and start tackling another problem. After a while, my head feels heavy, and I end up nodding off into a dream world.

Suddenly, an odd whistling sound disturbs the harmony of my cocoon. I barely have time to sit up before a head appears between the branches. It's Froo Win. The only one who knows about my hideout.

'Nyi Nyi[†]! I knew I'd find you here. Are you coming to play football?'

'No, not now. You know that I'm not allowed to play. I'd rather study.'

'Come on! Don't be a killjoy. The team needs you. We're training for the match with the neighbouring village. Aung Naing has twisted his ankle and we don't have enough players. Come on, catch that, you donkey.'

Froo Win throws the ball in the air; it skims the leaves of the highest branches and drops back down fast. I catch it and spin it on my finger for a few seconds. Even if he can't change my destiny for me, Froo Win always tries to include me in the group. Just for him, for his unwavering friendship and all the effort he makes, it will be worth the trouble that I'll get into. I clamber down the trunk of the tamarind tree. After all, I deserve this match.

† Habib's Burmese name.

12

The criminals

Dad does what he can to keep the shop stocked, and we survive from day to day. This month, he has managed to obtain a few boxes of aspirin from the nearest towns, Sittwe and Kyauktaw. He has also stocked up on fabric bags made by the elderly weaver women in Arakan. I stack all the items on our shelves. My stomach is rumbling again. I haven't eaten or drunk anything all day apart from a mug of black tea first thing in the morning. The soldiers are increasingly commandeering our food to supply their regiments, military camps, and units that are deployed in the region, which means mealtimes for us are fewer and farther between. Mum has promised to make us fried rice and curry this evening, which helps me to keep going even though dinner time is still a long way off.

It is an ordinary day in the shop. Dad has been treating headaches and bruises, and disinfecting wounds. I have made a few deliveries and managed to free up several hours to do maths revision in the back of the shop. Next to me, Babuli is concentrating hard as he copies out English words.

The market outside is bustling. Men and women from the surrounding mountains are advertising the quality of their freshly picked fruit and vegetables, while a bit further off, barge owners are haggling over the price of fish. Suddenly, the hubbub dies down, and the atmosphere turns oppressive at the sound of rhythmic steps approaching. I barely have time to look up before several soldiers, policemen, and high-ranking military intelligence officers storm into our shop. Two men sweep everything off the table where my father has his cash register and accounts book. Everything that he usually keeps meticulously tidy crashes onto the floor.

'Get out now and touch nothing.'

'What's going on?'

'Shut it, you dirty *kalar* pig! We have orders to investigate this shop.'

A soldier kicks Dad and hurls him outside before he has time to react. Arms wrench Babuli and me from our stools. I fly through the air and land on the beaten earth, grazed and crumpled. The captain shouts, 'Search everything!'

The men disperse and start ransacking all the drawers and shelves.

'Bring me the Bengali.'

My eyes are fixed on the military boots next to my head, and I don't dare look up.

'On your feet, you cretins!'

I grab Babuli's arm and we stand up trembling. While the officers vandalise the shop, other soldiers encircle it. They point their long rifles at us. Dad has been brought back inside and forced to his knees, with his hands behind his back, next to the captain. The crowd of gawping onlookers grows. They take the risk of asking the authorities, 'What have they done?'

They receive a frosty response: 'Move on! We are searching the *kalars*' shop.'

The people in the crowd are wary but insistent, keen to glean any information to feed the village rumour mills. A few officers, tired of waiting and enraged by the intrusive questions, distance themselves from the group and start questioning some of the more pushy members of the crowd.

'You, is this your shop? What do you sell here? Where did you buy the herbs?'

In a matter of seconds, the instinct for survival kicks in, and the mob disperses, leaving a large space around us.

Babuli clutches my shoulder. I can feel him shaking. I'm trying to listen to what's being said but can only catch snatches of conversation.

'And what's that?'

'Aspirin,' says Dad.

'Where did you get it? Who supplied it to you? What did you pay for it with? Foreign money?'

The interrogation lasts for several hours, during which time we aren't allowed to move or make a sound. The captain is humiliating my father. He pushes down on the back of his neck with his huge rigid boot and shouts at him as if he were a dog. His henchmen lay waste to the shop, and the chief of police orders his officers to assist.

'Collect all the evidence.'

The vandals seize three-quarters of the stock.

'We're going to search your house now. Move!'

They escort us to our hut where Mum is sitting on the ground next to the fire, stirring the rice. The chief of police enters ahead of us, yells and shakes her. The saucepan is knocked over and our meal spills on to the floor. I make a superhuman effort to choke back the tears that well up in my eyes.

'What are you doing? Have you hidden any drugs here?'

'I assure you sir, we are honest people. There is nothing here.'

The hut is turned upside down and looted. A few banknotes that my parents had removed from the hiding place to buy some fish and vegetables are confiscated. Nojum and Rohima look on in panic. We mustn't allow ourselves to become emotional as this would make the situation worse. We mustn't give them any reason to justify any more violence or looting.

The chief of police addresses our parents: 'You two *kalars*, you're coming with us. We're taking you to be interrogated. You're under arrest for possession of unauthorised products.'

Babuli, Rohima, Nojum, and I are rooted to the spot. Dad doesn't even have time to turn and look at us as he is dragged out by the guards. Mum just about manages to give us a hug and whisper in a strangled voice, 'My darlings ...'

'Enough of the blubbing, let's go.'

We stand with our arms dangling by our sides and don't budge from the doorstep for ten minutes. The soldiers have disappeared into thin air, taking our parents with them.

Our neighbours poke their heads hesitantly out of their houses. Two of the old women come up to us.

'Don't worry, little ones, they'll be back.'

Babuli breaks down.

'But where are they taking them?'

One of the women hugs him, and answers with a far-off look, 'To prison. At least it's not the military camp.'

I feel sick and feverish. The neighbour strokes my hair and

says in a kindly tone, 'Go inside, all of you. I'll bring you some rice for this evening. Pray for your parents. That will help them.'

I can't bring myself to go back inside straight away; the stench of violence is still hanging in the air. I leave Babuli with my sisters and run up the hillside to where you can see the prison, an old colonial building that has been converted into the rat hole that spreads terror throughout the valley. I loathe this country, where the biggest criminals — imposters in uniform — are constantly locking up innocent people and stripping them of everything. I vomit the little that remains in my stomach as I think of my parents at the mercy of these repugnant men. This feeling of powerlessness, of not being able to help them as an elder son should, drives me crazy. I collapse on the ground and vent my fury on the grass, desperately ripping up huge handfuls.

It is a miserable evening. We do our best to tidy everything and erase the memory of the vandals.

We are totally despondent and have no appetite as we huddle up together in the semi-darkness and pray that God will bring our parents back to us safe and sound. I've been crying so much that I've got hiccups. My sisters end up falling asleep on my lap, followed by Babuli who drops off too. I stay awake a little longer, praying in silence by candlelight, before finally dozing off, the last sob stuck in my throat.

I'm woken by the creaking of a wooden board. The sun is already high in the sky, blinding me. A shadow emerges in front of the hut door.

'Mum!'

My mother's smile fails to hide her tiredness and distress. She looks distraught, there are bags under her eyes and her hair is a mess. Her blouse is torn, and there's a big red mark on her neck. She takes us in her arms and breathes in the smell of our hair, one by one.

Dad enters the house an hour later, his face drawn with exhaustion. His eyebrow is bleeding, and his eye socket is purple; he hasn't been spared. I think I glimpse traces of cigarette burns on his arm. Our eyes briefly meet, but he is seeking out my mother. They throw themselves into one another's arms, then clasp each other's hands, which they lift up to their faces.

'What did they do to you, my darling?' Dad asks.

It takes a huge effort for Mum to get her words out. She gathers herself, inhales deeply, and stares at him before turning her head away.

'They asked me questions about you, about our business, about how we obtain our goods. If we leave the village, if we cross into the black zones. They strangled me several times to try and get me to admit wrongdoing.'

She remains quiet for a while, then in a broken voice says, 'They humiliated me. The president of the SLORC had a baton that he kept thrusting into me.'

Mum collapses into him. Dad grimaces in pain. He holds her tightly.

'I am so sorry that you had to go through all that. I feel bad that I couldn't protect you.'

Mum strokes his hands. Foreheads pressed against one another, they both cry in silence.

A lancing pain in his back forces Dad to lie down. He beckons to me and my brother and sisters. It is important that we listen to what he has to say.

'Twenty officers took turns to interrogate and hurt me. A so-called doctor asked me a whole lot of questions about the medicines that I use. Then the chief of police locked me up in a room alone with him. He walked round me, threatened me, hit me, and played with his pistol, saying that he would put a bullet in my head.'

Dad spreads his arms wide for us to snuggle up to him. He continues: 'My children, they try to justify the arrests by accusing us of all kinds of crimes that we haven't committed. Given our situation, they'll always find a pretext. I had to sign a paper to say that I exchanged kyats for foreign currency, which is strictly forbidden. I was also found guilty of possessing aspirin without authorisation. I admitted to all of this to appease them so that I would then be able to negotiate and pay for our freedom. If I hadn't done that, your mother and I wouldn't be here today. Our freedom is provisional and it has cost us dearly.

'From now on, we need to be beyond reproach, and we'll have to be careful. Our lives are on the line.'

13

Operation *Pyi Thaya*
(Clean and Beautiful Nation)

1991

Than Shwe launches Operation *Pyi Thaya*, Clean and Beautiful Nation, poetically named, like all the previous ethnic cleansing operations. The junta's soldiers are unleashed and set loose across the country, like rabid dogs. Tasked with erasing all traces of our presence, they pour into the plains and mountains of Arakan State where they patrol the towns and villages, shrieking '*Pyi Thaya*' with pride — just two words that justify the bloodshed, the flames that set our houses ablaze. They are seeking out the Rohingya, attempting to corner us, to eliminate our precious Muslim heritage. Myanmar, as Burma is now known, cannot conceive of any religious heritage other than Buddhism. Our mosques are a blot on the landscape of a nation that wants to sparkle with thousands of golden pagodas.

The soldiers conduct an unprecedented campaign of violence, under the orders of a new tyrant who is as narcissistic, bloodthirsty, and superstitious as the last one. Than Shwe likes to portray himself as the man who has covered the country's pagodas with gold leaf. It is his charitable offering to Buddha and his one-way ticket direct to Nirvana. The areas with the highest concentration of *kalars* are priority targets. The country must be cleansed of the unclean, who tarnish the kingdom of Buddha, so that the tyrant can guarantee his entry to Paradise. In the name of the great self-proclaimed master, Than Shwe, the golden man, the nation must be made clean and beautiful.

Hunting down the 'Bengali invaders' — the Rohingya, us — is a ritual that has been happening for decades in Myanmar. The lives of the 'parasites of the nation' are made more unbearable and miserable with each passing year, as the effort to eliminate the 'vermin', the 'black infidels', continues apace. Burials of our people are frequent.

Over the years, the names of the operations have become increasingly pompous and outlandish. In 1959, the army baptised the operation *Shwe Kyi* (Pure Gold). In 1966, it was *Kyi Gan* (Crow), followed by *Ngazinka* (Conqueror) and *Myat Mon* (More Purity) between 1967 and 1971. 1973 witnessed the launch of Operation *Major Aung Than* (Millions of Success), followed by *Sabae* (Purify and Whiten like the Jasmin Flower) a year later. From 1978 to 1979, the terrifying Operation *Nagamin* (Dragon King) was implemented, followed by many others. And finally in 1982, the despotic, irrevocable citizenship law. 'Rohingya' has become a forbidden word, never to be uttered, sentencing the men and women who bear this name to capital punishment.

Pure Gold, Dragon King, Purify and Whiten like the Jasmine Flower, and Clean and Beautiful Nation have all been manhunts, massacres with poetic, fanciful, warlike names that bestow glory on those who perpetrate them.

By cramming the Rohingya into prison cells, the idea that we are criminals has taken root. Our people live in reclusion in a state of apartheid in Arakan. We have been portrayed as an enemy who must be destroyed. This is a deliberate act by a dictator who has sought to sow hatred, fear, and disunity among the Burmese people. We are hostages who might one day throw off our chains and seek to rebel against our fate.

It is 1991 and Operation Clean and Beautiful Nation is at its height. Two hundred and sixty thousand Rohingya have already fled Arakan to seek refuge in Bangladesh. They are fleeing the army, which has been dispatched to the north of the region where arrests, forced labour, summary executions, acts of torture including rape, the burning of entire villages, and the demolition of mosques by soldiers are more and more frequent.

Across the whole of Arakan, the army is establishing model villages known as NaTaLa, built on land confiscated from the Rohingya. Robbed of all their possessions, the Rohingya are forced to abandon their land and homes, or to clear them to build new houses for the settlers from pure races, such as the Buddhist Rahkines and Bamars, who are often farmers, former Buddhist prisoners, or retired army officers and their families. Sometimes, these settlers are given *kalars* as slaves.

Sakkipara — also known as Thatkaybyin — the biggest Rohingya village near the city of Sittwe, is razed to the ground. It was the village of my maternal grandmother, who has been displaced to a wasteland called New Thatkaybyin. Hundreds of young men have been arrested and imprisoned for refusing to leave their homes.

The international community is compelled to react to the arrival of huge numbers of terrified men and women in Bangladesh. The United Nations Refugee Agency (UNHCR) negotiates with the Burmese and Bangladeshi governments to try to find a solution. A process of repatriation to Myanmar is implemented. For many, this is a forced deportation back to the hell that they have just fled.

14

Ethnic cleansing

I am 13 years old and I live in a world full of anguish. Sinister stories are passed around our community in whispers. Fear has become our daily lot. Soldiers and nationalist extremists continue the ethnic cleansing in Arakan State. Many Rohingya prefer to relinquish their birth names for safety reasons, but this is no guarantee. In Chin State, too, we are confined in small areas. We are worried, famished, and can no longer ignore the rumours.

Several miles from our village, in the former capital city of Mrauk U, part of an ancient empire built and inhabited by Muslims and Buddhists for centuries, the Muslim villages of Aung Daine and Nyung Pin Zay have been destroyed. Rohingya houses in the nearby village of Shit Taung along with the historic Shwe Dah Qazi Mosque have also been torn down.

There are no more Muslims on the jetty at Mrauk U, now completely cleared of shops, huts, and everyone who once traded there. The Rohingya who lived there have been displaced to the outskirts of a new village called Kwan Lon-Mandarabyin, where they are requisitioned for forced labour on the land that has been stolen from them.

Week after week, the bad news keeps coming with no respite. It is all terrifying. In August 1993, 18 Rohingya from Kyauktaw are arrested in Tangkup-Ann, handed over to the Rakhines by soldiers, and killed by blows from pickaxes after being forced to dig their own graves. Twelve Rohingya from Maungdaw are arrested in Pann-Mraung near Mrauk U by Regiment 377. They are executed.

We strive to keep the memory of these massacres alive.

15

The path of the innocents

A year later, in 1994, I hear that nearly 3,000 young Rohingya from Maungdaw have been arrested and executed by soldiers, including some of my distant cousins.

Who will tell the story of these massacres? The Rohingya do not have a written history. Our story could be told through the number of deaths, or the number of refugees, if only someone were counting. But the temporary camps in Kwan Lon, Aa Lae Zay, and Pon Na Mraung have been destroyed in an attempt to obliterate the little that remains to us, and to crush our will to resist and stand up for our rights. They want to eliminate everything that defines our identity. So it is that, in 1996, one of Arakan's most precious legacies is destroyed: the majestic mosque built in 1433 by the Muslim leader Sandhi Khan, who had come to offer help to King Naramaikhla of the great Mrauk U dynasty. The mosque was the ultimate proof of the history of Arakan, in particular the cohabitation of Muslims and Buddhists. It was an illustrious monument with a history that a superstitious and ultra-nationalistic government sought to deny. It was a memory that had to be erased so that the history of Arakan and Myanmar could be rewritten by those now in power.

Rohingya who have prayed all their lives in this mythical and mystical place are forced to dismantle each stone and each piece of teak and load it onto ox carts to be taken to the monastery in the Buddhist village of Shwe Taung. The mosque no longer exists, the slate is wiped clean, and history begins anew. The families from this ethnic group whose name cannot be spoken, the broken, starving families who have been deprived of everything, are then deported to Maungdaw. Those who refuse to go are arrested; some die of starvation in prison.

In Maungdaw, new arrivals pile into a town that has nothing to offer them and where they no longer have any rights. They are forbidden to marry, leave the town, or obtain any qualifications; they are deprived of an identity, and the number of births is restricted. Maungdaw is a prison for the innocent. The Rohingya are refused even the most basic human dignity.

The village is run by the special security force known as the NaSaKa. The soldiers prowl around, raping and stealing with impunity. They are accountable to no one. Any villager wishing to travel from one neighbourhood to another has to pay a tax. No Rohingya can leave these prison-towns unless they have specific authorisation that can only be bought with huge sums of money.

The NaSaKa spread terror among those whose name cannot be spoken, whose lives are made a living hell so that they will leave and go elsewhere, away from Myanmar. Those who stay are treated as slaves. Young people cannot afford the marriage permits, and unmarried couples are imprisoned for years in filthy cells, poor innocent 'criminals' incarcerated in the dictator's jails alongside those other innocents, the political prisoners.

16

The trespassers

I often wish I could stop time and remain the carefree child who is vanishing fast with each passing month. I cling on to Dad as we watch 14 men hobble along, feet chained, surrounded by soldiers. They are all friends of my father's except for two Chins who he has never seen before.

Our local blacksmith whispers to his wife, who is visibly distressed by the spectacle, 'I can't bear to see my cousin being taken away like that.'

'We can't do anything more for them. They are condemned men.'

'May God be with them.'

A neighbour emerges from his hut and joins us.

'What's happening? I know them, they're from my village.'

'The poor beggars were arrested in the jungle near Roukchaung while attempting to escape Arakan.'

'The black zone, always this damn black zone. Arakan may

be our home but it's not safe for us here. Whenever we set a foot outside the village, they're on to us. We're penned in like animals.'

'They're taking them to U Myo Khin's military intelligence bureau in Kyauktaw. He is an evil man. They have no hope.'

'Is it better to die or be crammed into their prisons?'

A few days later, Hafzaw, a family friend, comes over for tea. He slumps down and buries his face in his hands.

'I was walking through the jungle on my way home and I saw them in the distance. I stopped stock-still. I was terrified. They made them kneel. Colonel Aung Kyaw Thein and the deputy commander of Roukchaung murdered them one by one with a bullet to the back of the head. They fell into the holes that they had just dug.'

Ordinary mass graves into which the Rohingya disappear without history noticing.

The persecutions continue and in the midst of it all my little sister Habibah is born, a ray of light in this miserable daily existence.

17

The army's urinals

Days and months pass, and the situation continues to deteriorate. Young soldiers, less vicious than the higher ranks, but not lacking in persistence, continually come by Dad's shop to demand money or gifts. They help themselves to soap, sandals, and bags.

The news from rest of the region is not good. The arbitrary arrests intensify. Captain ABN has replaced Captain KZW and, shortly after his posting to the village, turns up uninvited at our house.

'Your land has been designated as the site for the regiment's latrines.'

Once again, they are trying to reduce our dwelling to a shithouse. In a state of shock, my father draws himself up to his full height, determined to stand up to the man.

'No, I have the right to live here. I have federal authority approval.'

'Do you have the deeds?'

'Who has deeds in the Chin mountains? Only towns in the plains and cities grant title deeds. No authority gives deeds here, not even in the ethnic zones. No villager here has any, you know that as well as I do.'

'Your house has been built on land with no title deeds so it will be demolished and the land will revert to the state. We have already done you the favour of allowing you to live here all this time.'

'If my house is to be destroyed, the SLORC office in the village should follow, because there are no title deeds anywhere in this state.'

The captain becomes more and more aggressive. He kicks over the low table, knocking papers, cups, and tea to the ground.

'Don't try and be clever with me, *kalar*, or I'll make you disappear well before your house.'

I can feel goosebumps all over my body. I don't want him to touch Dad.

The Christian priest, with whom Dad has a good relationship, comes to see us that evening, after Mum informs him what has happened.

'It's us they are after, the land is just a pretext. What will become of my children if we stay here?' says my father.

'Listen, things are reaching a critical point in the village. I can negotiate with the captain to put our presbytery here instead of the latrines, although of course there are no guarantees. You must leave the village before you get into even bigger trouble. The church will buy your house and your land — I can offer you eighty thousand kyats. That will help pay for the journey.'

It takes Dad 24 hours to decide to leave everything behind; he knows that our lives are on the line and that our house is already lost. He thanks the priest for his offer and reluctantly accepts.

18

The undesirables

I am 15 years old and wonder if I'll ever reach adulthood or if I'll be murdered first. So many young Rohingya men are disappearing. I try not to think about it. Even though the future seems uncertain and threatening for our family, I put all my energy into concentrating on my schoolwork. I want to give Dad hope and comfort him with my good results. I haven't allowed myself to go out and play for a long time now. He wants his children to be lawyers, and making his dream come true would be the ultimate achievement. Whatever the obstacles, I want to excel in the subjects that will give me access to further education. Those subjects are maths, physics, biology, and chemistry, and I quickly realise that English is important too. I devour all the information I can. I study, recite, read, and calculate for as long as the candlelight allows.

Two weeks before the captain showed up at our house, the marketplace was destroyed by fire. Panicked villagers tried to fight it, but it spread to houses, huts, and shops. Buckets of water, earth, and sand were flying in all directions in the desperate attempt to extinguish it. Now all that remains is a huge pile of ashes. Seven houses and the village shop where Froo Win and I watched a movie once also burnt down. We don't know how it started. The authorities began interrogating the locals who were present, but most of us dispersed to avoid trouble. From our camp above the village, I saw the soldiers take away 20 people.

Dad decides to liquidate the shop. Organising our departure requires many permits. Leaving the village is a crime, even though we have effectively been evicted from our house. We will need to travel through black zones that are forbidden to Muslims. My father has to give the army 50,000 of the 80,000 kyats that the church has paid us in order to obtain the necessary authorisations to leave.

We take with us what we can, including crockery and cooking implements, unsold products from the shop, official identity documents and cards, and our old title deeds, which Dad carefully preserves despite the scant value the authorities place on them.

I haven't seen Froo Win for a long time, either around the village or in the places where we used to meet up when we had some free time. This saddens me. I would like to say goodbye to him, but my parents have repeatedly told us not to go out, and Froo Win doesn't come round to my house anymore.

We load up a small motorboat. It is an enforced and definitive farewell to my childhood village. I look at the reflection of the little village on the still waters of the river, an image that imprints itself on my memory, part of my personal history.

The motor starts to hum. The wave caused by the boat moving on the water erases the reflection of the huts, the people, and the school as we set off into the unknown. I stare at the village with a heavy heart until it vanishes in the mist. I hear a few last shouts from the children left behind in the playground, and then everything goes quiet, probably because our kindly teachers have called for silence. I hear the deep steady tones of my teacher Saya Naing. Then nothing. New landscapes slide by along the riverbank as the boat transports me to a world of plains and deltas. My brother lies cradled in Mum's arms, playing with some sticks. Mum is keeping an eye on Habibah, Nojum, and Rohima who are sleeping under a jute sack that has been hung up to create some shade. Dad sits bolt upright next to the motor on the left of the skipper. His fists are clenched, his jaw rigid with worry, but he remains stoic. He is focusing on the horizon. I take him a cup of water. He stares at me for a second and smiles briefly as he puts his arm around me and draws my head into his chest. I can feel his anguish, despite his deliberately impassive stance. We are travelling towards the heart of Arakan State, straight into the lion's den, where tormenting the Rohingya has become a national sport; the region that my family has been fleeing forever, but is the only place where we can legally live, where we have family ties and property.

Behind us, the hut where we have spent our childhoods, the fruit of my parents' love and work, has been abandoned because of hatred and a cruel callous power. Memories of the terrifying tales of Arakan spin round in my head. Grandma's ghosts come back to me. Is this where they catch up with us?

The day is made even more unbearable because the further we go, the more we fear that this is a journey of no return. Whatever happens, this enforced departure does not bode well.

It will take us 48 hours to reach our destination. All we have had to eat is a few mouthfuls of rice. When the sun eventually sets on the first day, we are halfway there. We moor the boat at the jetty of a bustling town and remain in the port, sleeping piled up on top of one another.

I wake up several times, and soon the moon appears in the sky. Our home may be destroyed, our hills and mountainsides may be forbidden territory, but no one can take the moon away from us — pure, serene, reassuring, and loyal. It makes the darkness more bearable.

At dawn, the motor chugs into action, arousing me from strange dreams full of the unknown. We continue travelling along the river. Dark-skinned men on small wooden barges drift by, hauling on multicoloured sails made from torn jute sacks and shredded drapes. They look like Rohingya, but their stories are a mystery to me. Are they fleeing like us? Our paths cross as we travel the river to our respective destinies. Further on, other men float along on gigantic bamboo rafts built for transporting the canes that they will most likely trade in Sittwe.

In the distance, Mrauk U stands out from the plain with its age-old temples, symbols of the period up to 1784 when Arakan was an independent empire. Mrauk U is the former capital of Rohang, since renamed Arakan. It was there that our Rohingya and Rakhine ancestors lived together peacefully.

The waterway on which we are travelling is a complex and dangerous maze. Dad says that if you don't know your way around and you head into the wrong tributary, you risk getting lost and might never come out. It is this interlinking mass of waterways that once protected the kingdom of Rohang.

The river served as a rampart against the kingdom's enemies, which included the kings of the neighbouring country, Burma. Arakan was a land of Buddhists and Muslims, with many pagodas and mosques, and was independent before it was colonised by the Burmese, then the British. Today, Burma, now Myanmar, has annexed Arakan and made it one of the country's main regions. The nation profits from its natural resources, but rejects its original people: us.

It is on these Arakan plains, between the old Buddhist temples, that the solemn, grandiose, and sacred mosque of Sandhi Khan, described by Grandma as a haven of peace and a soothing place of refuge, once rose. The men, women, and children of Arakan used to come to the mosque to dream and pray. Many tears were shed, and many hopes were cherished on its stones. Carefree children once played in its courtyard. Then Sandhi Khan was erased from the landscape, destroyed stone by stone by the intolerance of Buddhist extremists. Its destruction also brought down the bridge that linked these two cultures once bound by a shared land and history.

My mind drifts as we pass across these fertile and abundant lands, towards the mystery that awaits us in the port of Sittwe, the new capital, where Granny, my maternal grandmother, lives. I imagine the big ponds in which Granny breeds the fish and prawns that Mum has often told me about.

Dad comes to sit beside me and says, 'Son, life in Sittwe will be different. The tensions between ethnic groups are much worse than in our village. We will be watched closely, but we will do all we can to make sure that you can carry on studying for as long as possible. Although the city is hostile to Muslims, it has the best schools in Arakan.'

I look at him as a smile forms in the corners of his mouth. I won't disappoint him. In the distance, we can see the huge bay and port of Sittwe. We watch fishermen returning from the sea. As each fishing boat comes into port, men, women, and children race towards it in the hope of getting their hands on a fish to sell at the market — the commission that they earn from a sale will ensure their survival that day. In the midst of all this hubbub, we draw alongside the jetty between some houses on stilts. The authorities have a guard post there. We start unloading and are immediately taken to one side to pay special taxes and be questioned about the legitimacy of our journey.

19

The taste of salt

We move to New Thatkaybyin, close to where Mum was born. It is on the outskirts of Sittwe, where nearly all the city's Muslim neighbourhoods, except Minghala, are located. On arrival, I discover that Granny's so-called abundant ponds in her backyard are actually really small, with just a few fish swimming around, which she sells at the market or occasionally fries up to eat. I soon find out that the house where Mum used to live in Thatkaybyin is now part of Military Training Camp 313, where Rohingya and other prisoners are interrogated and tortured. The population of Thatkaybyin has been relocated eight miles away to New Thatkaybyin, which is where Granny now lives.

The original village was ransacked during Operation Clean and Beautiful Nation, in which every house was searched, and hundreds of villagers, including some of my uncles, cousins, and mother's friends, were interrogated and arrested, while others were forced to surrender their property or pay fines. Some disappeared, always for the same crime of simply existing.

The authorities make families submit an official list of family members that allows them to monitor the movements of every person in every household as they patrol our neighbourhoods. If a family member fails to return home before curfew, he or she is arrested. If someone disappears, the whole family suffers. We are now registered on Granny's family list and, every evening, we have to be back in her hut before sunset. They are keeping a close watch on us.

Besides her small fish farm, Granny grows a few vegetables that she trades at the morning market. I become acquainted with new uncles, aunts, and cousins to whom I am closely or distantly related. They all welcome us warmly and bombard us with recommendations and explanations about what to expect from this new life.

'Avoid the Kyaungdalan neighbourhood. Three gangs of young Rakhines regularly assault Rohingya there.'

'May God protect us, our old mosque is still just about standing, but every day a member of the family is sent to help build the cultural museum on land that belongs to the mosque. How long before it's reduced to rubble?'

'The local authorities have begun a major building project for the Buddhists, the Lawkananda pagoda. They're extremely proud of it. They recruit us to carry bricks and sacks of cement, or force us to make donations towards the building work.'

'What are you going to do about your sons? They are clever boys. You could send them to a religious school. No one will bother them there and they won't be bullied by the teachers or the other students.'

Dad makes it clear that his decision is made — a state school.

'They are strong enough not to let it upset them. I want my children to enjoy the same education as other Burmese children. It's their right.'

I notice that there is not the same camaraderie between ethnic groups as there was in my village. The Rakhines are the majority here. There are no Chins, Khumis, or other minorities. The kind of diversity that encourages tolerance does not exist. The Rakhines' nationalist pride and religious extremism creates a climate of fear, and frequent harassment and bullying add to the dangers already posed by the authorities and the army, in particular the NaSaKa. Like other Rohingya, I quickly learn to avoid the Rakhine neighbourhoods, where we are exposed to insults and threats, and where the total impunity that reigns often puts our lives at risk. As the Rakhines see it, beating a Rohingya is no more reprehensible than thrashing a defenceless animal. Taking the long way round becomes a routine security measure.

Dad gets it into his head that he wants to grow crops on the last plots of land for which Grandma, my paternal grandmother, still holds the deeds. He has borrowed some gardening tools and plans to go there in a few days' time to dig over the soil and plant his seeds. This will enable him to feed his family. The plot of land in question is close to Granny's house, in the Nazi district, named after the former Rohingya village chief Nazirahm.

Then comes news from on high, as if destiny itself were against us: the local authorities are prohibiting the planting of crops and confiscating any land used for growing them.

Despite the efforts of relatives to dissuade him, in desperation my father decides to file a complaint. Several days later, he is called to the ASPDC[†]. He gathers together the old papers that he keeps carefully in a plastic wallet.

I ask him, 'Why didn't you have papers for our house in Mylmin?'

'Title deeds are rare in ethnic regions, Habib, but they are more common in large urban areas like Sittwe, Yangon, and Mandalay. It is a system that was introduced by the English. Nowadays, these are the only papers that we can use to prove that we have certain rights, and the soldiers cannot simply ignore the ones that I've got here. They may be nasty and vicious, but when it comes to constitutional laws, they have to think twice before disregarding them.'

I go with him to the local authority office and wait on the bench outside. I can hear the conversation through the window.

'The land that you are laying claim to in the Nazi district has been sold for the benefit of the state and the people of Myanmar. It is public property and will be used for the nation.'

'So the law does not apply here? You represent the state. You understand the meaning of the law and the value of my title deeds.'

'We are the law here! Do you understand?'

'I make just one request. Take the land but keep my father's name on the title deeds.'

'Have you got no brains?! Do you want to spend the rest of your life in prison like that other *kalar*, Hla Aung, the so-called lawyer? Get out of my office now and don't come back bothering me with your whining or it will be straight to jail for you!'

This is followed by a long silence. Dad emerges from the office, his face betraying a combination of anger and disappointment. We head back to the village.

---

† Arakan State Peace and Development Council.

Despite my family's financial difficulties, Dad introduces me and my brother to the headmaster for enrolment in secondary school, and he applies to enrol my little sisters in the primary school. It costs a lot of money, and the other Rohingya don't understand why my father is so determined to send us to a school where abuse and humiliation will be major obstacles to our learning. With the constant taxes, property confiscations, and arrests, sending us to school is not only an extra expense, but also more money that needs to be earned.

My brother and I are given some work at a small youth hostel. We sell bus tickets and write letters and special dispensation requests for Rohingya wishing to travel outside Sittwe. I also help those who have managed to obtain temporary permits to leave Maungdaw in the far north of Arakan. They have travelled huge distances in the hope of finding a solution for their various desperate situations, mostly involving buying medicines for a dying relative or telephoning family members in exile, begging them to send money. The fact that my brother and I speak Rohingya, Rakhine, and Burmese fluently means that we can sell our services and, at the same time, be useful to our community. In Arakan, only Muslims are required to obtain travel permits. Completed documents must be presented in person at 11 different administrative offices around town. Each official's palm is greased in exchange for his stamp, standard everyday bribes without which the temporary travel permit for 'Bengalis' is rejected. Rohingya are scared of doing this themselves because dealing directly with the authorities always entails an element of risk. Without these documents, it is impossible to leave the village, even to visit a sick relative in Arakan, the same region. Babuli and I are beginning to understand how the system works and how to approach officials.

After running from one office to another the whole morning, I take a short break in a small teahouse where the owner provides a Thermos free of charge. Three adult Rakhines come in. They deliberately bump into me before sitting down at a little table next to mine and launching into a vehement diatribe.

'In the past, my grandfather used to chop *kalars*' heads off, but they breed quickly, those mongrels.'

'They come here and convert our women. They marry four at once, and then they knock them up! It's like the plague, it spreads. The problem needs to be nipped in the bud before we get totally invaded.'

'Rakhines are the descendants of the King of Arakan. We mustn't forget that. It's high time that we did a real cleansing operation instead of sitting back and letting ourselves be invaded.'

'They've already had enough hospitality from us. They've even stolen the shade from our trees and our houses.'

I've got used to this kind of lunacy, but still my blood boils every time I hear it and I'm filled with disgust. I don't feel hatred, because I understood a long time ago that hate serves no purpose, it is just stupid and belittling to those who feel it. My instinct for survival kicks in. Nothing that I could say or do would make me prevail in this situation. I have to move carefully to prepare an escape route so that these imbeciles don't find some excuse to get carried away, which could be disastrous for me.

They pretend that they haven't noticed me until one of them prods me with his finger.

'Hey, *kalar*, are you listening?'

I shift away a little, and try to behave as if nothing has happened. He puts the finger that he has just used to prod me in his mouth.

'*Kalars* are like salt for us. We're going to dissolve you on our tongues until there's nothing left of you.'

Just as I stand to make my escape, the three men launch themselves at me. The punches fly. I pick myself up without retaliating and quickly make myself scarce, aching all over, with a shooting pain in my ribs.

Eventually, Babuli and I are accepted by the school. Dad has done what needed to be done. There are thousands of students, but only four of us are Muslims. When we enter the building for the first time we're met with contemptuous and hostile looks. We have to act meek. We carry on walking, pretending to be impervious to the sneering. We quickly get into the habit of not hanging around in certain isolated places or empty corridors.

I concentrate on my lessons and my studies. As the weeks go by, my classmates become less unpleasant than those in other classes. Some even reply politely when I take the risk of asking them for some extra information that I need. However, I'm scared of the breaks, and of class outings where every opportunity is taken to shove, insult, or hit me. Although it is obvious that the Rakhine and Bamar teachers feel repulsion and animosity towards me, they do sometimes intervene when I am being jostled and knocked about in the corridors or the playground. The boys are the most vindictive. The girls tend to stay on the sidelines, making fun of my eyebrows, nose, and skin colour.

I learn to distance myself from it all, to ignore the insults, turn a deaf ear to the racist comments, and apply myself to my homework so that none of the teachers has any reason to complain about my behaviour or my results. I attend all the classes, pay attention to every single explanation, and prefer to offer my classmates help rather than count on theirs.

I am always anxious about leaving school at the end of the day. I rush to get to my job at the youth hostel, but I am often waylaid and treated harshly by the other students before managing to escape.

I can't help slowing down whenever I pass a football match, although I always keep my distance on the other side of the street. I'm longing to kick the ball, but no Rohingya plays football in Sittwe, and joining any of the Rakhine teams is unimaginable. Life in Sittwe leaves a sour taste in the mouth. It's best not to fall sick because the nurses in the hospital treat us with disgust, if indeed they deign to treat us at all. There are continual persecutions outside mosques in the Nazi, Aung Minghala, and Zaygyi districts. Young Rakhines and monks throw projectiles into the neighbourhood shops.

The disappearances affect us all. Since 1993, thousands of Rohingya have disappeared, particularly in and around Maungdaw and Buthidaung, townships where apartheid is a reality. These are places where the Rohingya are excluded from everything including trade, communication, and access to education and medical treatment, imprisoned by poverty and controlled by the fearsome NaSaKa. All those arrested disappear. Will they ever come back? Arbitrary executions in the forest are standard practice in the black zones. Rohingya die and no one counts the number of dead, the disappeared, or the mass graves.

One evening, a man enters our hut. Mum stands up, the emotion showing on her face. It's her cousin Ahmed. She grasps his hands and pulls them to her face. He sits down beside us.

He is skin and bone, clearly very weak, and unable to focus. He is barely 30 years old but looks like an old man. Ahmed has spent seven years in prison and has just been released this week, along with some others. Seven years in prison for breaking the law by leaving his village without the damn document that is so hard to obtain. He tells us that the others were arrested while travelling by car from Maungdaw to Sittwe, or by bus or boat to Yangon, or because they were denounced by neighbours or caught during a night raid shortly after reaching their destinations.

Seven years of hell for attempting to flee an apartheid state where Rohingya just wait to die. Many do not survive captivity, but no figures exist for prison deaths. The corpses are removed from cells and probably thrown somewhere with all the others, like carrion.

Hundreds of men like Ahmed continue to be detained every month for daring to cross the barrier of the enclosures in which we are confined. Ahmed breaks down in tears, unable to say any more.

After dozing for a few hours, he manages to whisper a few words that evening: 'I'd reached Yangon when they arrested me. I thought I was finally safe and would manage to pass unnoticed in the crowd. But they have informers everywhere. I spent six months in prison there before they sent me to Sittwe. Death would have been preferable to what we endured, and it will catch up with us soon anyway. God protect all our brothers and sisters who are still there. I often hoped that death would take me.'

With trembling hands, he sets his soup bowl down and shuffles back to his sister's house before night falls. The authorities have registered him on the family list there and he must return every evening for the army's spot checks.

At night, I'm haunted by thoughts of prison cells. I shudder at the thought of being locked up and tortured one day like all the others. I mustn't think about it.

Some mornings, trucks come to the Muslim districts of Sittwe to take men and women to do forced labour for a day, a week, or sometimes, for the unluckiest, up to a month. They are put to work building extensions to military camps, and digging holes and fish ponds for the soldiers who blockade our villages. My cousins, uncles, and aunts are all regularly conscripted. Those of us who are not requisitioned work to eat and are careful to be back before sunset.

We avoid talking about the personal degradation and humiliation to which the soldiers subject us. Remembering them is a form of torture in itself, and talking about them would be to re-live the humiliation and make our community all the more fragile by exacerbating our servitude. What's the point of having witnesses and people to tell our story? Is there anyone who really cares about changing our fate? We just have to accept it, and keep our heads high in order to survive and progress one step at a time, in the present.

At night, I sleep near Dad. He removes his radio from its hiding place under the floorboard and switches it on, keeping the sound low so the neighbours can't hear. We pick up the BBC and Voice of America in Burmese, and listen for as long as we can stay awake. The outside world. I find that I am increasingly questioning our life and the lives of others. How does the dictator manage to silence a whole people so effectively? There are thousands of us against one tyrant. My father believes that the only way to topple the regime is through a union of all peoples in this nation of many ethnic groups.

If I am to pass my exams, I need private lessons to supplement what I'm learning in school. That's how many teachers manage to earn a decent salary. My close relatives have clubbed together and I've got almost enough now for three extracurricular lessons a week. The challenge is to find a teacher who will take me on, Dad says. He murmurs a few encouraging words as he straightens the collar of my shirt. We've drawn up a list of the most broad-minded teachers whom I will approach in the first instance.

The low literacy rate in our community, and the regularity of random taxes, have made it almost impossible for Rohingya — teachers or students — to participate in the education system. Too few Rohingya students have access to schooling and no Rakhine would even consider attending lessons given by a Muslim, however qualified he or she may be.

On this particular Friday morning, in November 1996, I put on my white shirt that I save for special occasions, a gift from Mum. I pull on a spotless *longyi* and carefully brush my hair. I look smart. Now all I need to complete the look is an exercise book and pencil to show how conscientious I am. I cycle to the central market in Sittwe, which is buzzing with people. Only Rakhines are allowed to use the main aisles, the few Rohingya women are restricted to the far corners of the market. I quickly purchase an exercise book from a Rakhine trader and am about to pedal off when four boys block my route. I change direction and turn back towards the dense crowd but struggle to give them the slip. One of them grabs my arm, another taps me on the head. I try to break free from their grip, but they become more and more threatening and force me into a quiet corner.

'Do you like it here in our country, little *kalar*?'

'The lesson that our grandparents gave yours wasn't enough then? You're not worried about losing your head?'

They push me into a heap of rotting waste in a narrow back alley. I pick myself up, and manage to dodge under a stall and run towards the place where I left my bike without turning to check whether they are still behind me. I shake them off, but have to go home to change and clean myself up before setting off in search of a teacher for my extra lessons.

At the first school, a few students are milling around outside the classroom. I ask to see the teacher.

'What do you want from him? We don't accept *kalars* here.'

Before I have time to respond, the teacher enters the classroom. I rush up to him and address him courteously as his status requires.

'Good morning sir. May I present my respects? I was told that you still have places for extracurricular lessons.'

The other students are listening and giving the teacher the evil eye. He replies coldly and with obvious discomfort, 'Sorry, you've been told wrong, we don't take black Muslims here.'

I don't insist.

'Goodbye, ten per cent,' shouts one of the students.

This is another derogatory term, used to imply that we are only ten per cent human, not worthy of respect, of no value.

I swallow my pride, straddle my bike, and leave. It is a thankless task. All the extracurricular classes in the city centre are closed to me. These are the most popular and are considered the best. Teachers aren't short of requests from students and can happily reject my application. Some of them categorically refuse me entry to the building. Others hesitate and prefer to ask for the approval of their Rakhine students.

I am eventually accepted for maths and physics classes by two lesser-known teachers. Although my presence is barely tolerated by the other students, they also want to help their teacher to make ends meet and therefore give their approval. I stay at the back of the classroom and they mostly forget that I am there.

When I have a little free time, I go off on my bike to a banyan tree I've discovered, which becomes my new hideout. Its long, thick branches give me somewhere private to study where I can recite my lessons early in the morning. At weekends, I am hidden from view up in the tree and am able to watch at my leisure some of the football matches between the Rakhine teams.

One particular Saturday as I am pedalling towards my tree, my attention is drawn to a turn-off where a dozen prisoners are breaking stones. They are chained together by their feet and are wearing soiled, threadbare white uniforms. Their bodies are gaunt and broken, souls clinging to life. That could be me, my brother, or my father. Could I bear the idea of such suffering with no apparent end? Something makes me stop. I put my bike down on the ground to be able to watch them more closely. My heart leaps. It's him: Froo Win! Four policemen are guarding the convicts. The joy of seeing my friend again makes me ignore all possible danger. I go up to the officers, forgetting my black skin and the word 'Muslim' engraved on my forehead. I approach with my hands held out towards them bearing the fritters and fried rice that I'm taking to my grandmother at the market.

'Please, sirs, I would like to speak to one of your prisoners, I've just recognised him, we used to play together when we were children.'

They look at my offerings with interest and snatch them up hungrily.

'Go on. You've got five minutes.'

When he sees me, Froo Win's emaciated face lights up. We can't hug or touch one another, but our smiles communicate the huge pleasure of seeing each other again.

'Nyi Nyi! You live here now?' he says in a frail voice.

'Yes, they had to put in some toilet blocks for the soldiers in the village. They couldn't hold it in any longer.'

I wink at him knowingly. He attempts a grimace. I ask him the burning question: 'What happened to you? I didn't see you when I left Mylmin.'

'I was arrested on the day of the fire in the video shop, the police were trying to find out how it started, and they arrested everybody there, including me. It was probably a short circuit in the projection room. I was sentenced to three years in prison because I was a minor and I shouldn't have been there. I was transferred to Sittwe and we have to do hard labour nearly every day. I can't take it anymore.'

Froo Win is emaciated and his cheeks are sunken. His lovely pink complexion, which I used to tease him about, is now grey. The light in his eyes is extinguished.

One of the policeman stands up. The five minutes are over.

'Be brave, my brother, keep going.'

I leave without daring to look back. Behind me, the sound of spades rings out louder than ever.

The end of the year approaches. I've planned my revision schedule.

One day, as I am making my way along the path towards my hideout, three soldiers order me to stop.

'Put your bike down, you filthy *kalar*.'

'What are you doing, Bengali? Going for a little outing?'

'Crouch down and jump like a frog to the end of the road and back.'

Dad has taught me to be submissive and play by their rules. I do as they say. They guffaw loudly. I just have to deal with it, it's an uncomfortable moment and it'll pass. They insult me and I sense the impending danger. When I get back to where they are standing, and once they've stopped laughing, they make me sweep the leaves around their military base. They keep me there for another two hours.

Episodes like this are a regular occurrence, I either have to do press-ups in front of them, or stand on one foot. It gives these soldiers who lack any shred of humanity the opportunity to abuse others and have a good laugh.

I try to take other routes into the city centre, but the options are limited. The Rakhine neighbourhoods where the ultra-nationalists hang out and the military camps surrounding the Rohingya villages are difficult to avoid.

In December 1996, there are demonstrations by students and opponents of the regime in universities across Myanmar. These are met with anxiety but also hope that the dictatorship will be weakened once and for all. The government cuts off our electricity, water, and telephone lines. For three days, Sittwe is more isolated from the world than ever. Soldiers patrol the Muslim villages of Nazi, Mawleik, and Pharagyi, and Sittwe market. The curfew is bought forward and the city's university closed. The junta decrees martial law. Any gathering of more than three people after eight o'clock in the evening is strictly forbidden for all ethnic groups in Myanmar, and it's difficult to buy anything as prices soar. It is dangerous for us to go out, so we only do so when strictly necessary, and even then many of us are attacked and robbed in broad daylight. I stay at home as much as possible, revising for my final exams, and I am hungry most of the time.

20

The tree's memory

Construction of the new Arakan cultural centre on land confiscated from the old mosque in Sittwe is almost complete. History will be revised here; people will be told that Arakan has always been a Buddhist state. No mention will be made of Sandhi Khan. No document will attest to the presence of Muslims on these lands. The official version of Arakan history is a lie that grows over the years with the erection of pagodas, the destruction of mosques, the publication of Rakhine history books that omit any mention of the Rohingya, and now this museum.

Dad has found out that the government has divided his father's land into several lots and put them up for sale. He wants to show me them before they are covered in concrete and occupied by soldiers. I have just turned 17 and it is important to him that I am aware of my origins, of our property and what has been stolen from us, everything that is part of our family history, deeply rooted in Arakan. He says to me sadly, 'This should have been your inheritance. This is what I wanted to leave you and your children.'

Night is falling fast, and there is no time to lose. The land is located between the Nazi district and Sittwe city centre. At the start of a path into the fields, we stop next to a tree that is home to hundreds of bats.

'This tree has always been very precious to me. It's a living memory. It saw me grow up and it watched my great-grandparents working the land. They were highly respected, because they knew how to fertilise and plough the land better than anyone. They taught us to love and look after this land, and in return it kept us alive.'

A roar disturbs the silence. Three men are running towards us. Police. Dad grabs me by the wrists and whispers in my ear, 'Whatever happens, Habib, do not say that this land was ours.'

One of them draws level with us.

'On the ground, now, *kalars*!'

We do as he says.

'This land belongs to the state. Entry is forbidden. What are you doing here, you dirty thieves?'

Dad bites his lip.

'Excuse us. We worked hard today. We wanted to get home quickly.'

'Shut it, parasite. Who do you think you are? Just because we let you live here, you think you can put your filthy *kalar* feet wherever you like, contaminating other people's land?'

The policeman turns to his colleagues. 'I'll fetch the jeep. You two, keep an eye on them.'

As he walks off, his two colleagues keep us kneeling in front of them. I feel a violent blow to my back and am pinned to the floor. Dad disappears from my field of vision. I can't hear anything. The right side of my face is shoved into the mud and a boot stamps on my left ear. I take a kick to the stomach, and others to my calves. They are really going for it. I don't know which way to curl up. I feel the lacerations on my skin, the blood pouring down my skull, and am overcome by nausea.

The jeep arrives. Two policeman jump out and handcuff our hands behind our backs. They haul us up by the shoulders and throw us into the back. A boot crashes into my face again. The tastes of mud and blood combine in my mouth. The engine starts.

'Take them to Station 1 next to the central market where they'll be interrogated.'

21

Pandemonium

The gates of Sittwe's main prison open. The jeep enters the courtyard. A glance at Dad brings the blows raining down on me. I shudder, utterly panic-stricken. My heart is hammering at a hundred miles an hour. I stare at the ground. I must not let my emotions show. We are thrown out of the vehicle and taken to the cells.

'We've got some new pals for you.'

The policeman pushes us into a cell of around 40 square metres, which is crammed with 50 or so prisoners. Many are hunched in uncomfortable positions. A patch of floor is soiled with urine and spit; the foul, stinking air makes for a toxic atmosphere. The prisoners protest and grumble at our arrival, hatred in their eyes. We have barely entered the cell before kicks to our legs force us to crouch down and try to find a space somewhere in among them. There is clearly no room for anyone else and we are two too many.

One of the prisoners, a Rakhine, flashes us a broad, terrifying smile revealing gums and yellowing teeth worn down by years of chewing betel leaf and slaked lime. He spits a ball of red phlegm onto the feet of another prisoner who bends over to wipe it off, without flinching. Two prisoners are using a jute sack to fan him. Sitting cross-legged, he runs his tongue over his suppurating lips, points at us, and growls.

'Look, here are two *kalars* that we can make short work of. Bring them to me.'

The prisoners closest to the cell's door push us towards him; the others grumble and begrudgingly move aside to make room for us. I can read my father's thoughts. He must be saying to himself, we are the only Rohingya in this cell full of Rakhines and if we don't come up with something quickly, we are not going to survive. The man who called us over makes us kneel in front of him. I find him repugnant. He leans on the wall, legs akimbo, scratching his private parts, and says, 'I give the orders around here, you will respect me and you will follow the rules of the cell.'

He grabs a prisoner's ear and shoves the man's head to the ground. He crushes it under his grubby foot and then punches him in the face and ribs.

'That's what you've got coming to you if you disobey me. That's the punishment. There is work to be done to keep this stinking hole in the back end of Burma looked after and we are in need of some entertainment round here, aren't we boys? You two *kalars* have turned up at just the right time.'

A handful of prisoners snigger, cough, and scratch their bodies and genitals. Others lower their eyes, exhausted, barely conscious, numbed by the heat or the pain.

Behind the bars, the policemen guarding the cell watch

the scene out of the corner of their eyes, saying nothing. They remain impassive, with just an occasional mocking grimace. It's an amusing spectacle for men short on action.

The Rahkine continues: 'We sleep and clean the cell when I say so. And, once a day, you take it in turns to massage me like this. Kyaw!'

A prisoner rushes over and kneads his shoulders.

'Aaah! That feels good ...'

He seems to drift off for a few seconds, closing his eyes to enjoy the pleasure of the massage, before abruptly recovering his senses.

'Sometimes I just need to unwind a bit. Now, *kalar*, sit there. If you're not happy, you can fight. We like bets. But perhaps you have something to offer me.'

The man belches and cracks his fingers as he stares defiantly at Dad before spitting at him.

I am intimidated and sickened by this savage. I imagine that Dad must be thinking that only money can assuage their hatred. Otherwise they're going to destroy us.

With immense calm, Dad turns towards the Rahkine.

'Show us some clemency, allow us to have a dry space in the cell tonight. Leave me and my son alone. My wife will have been informed and will soon be bringing some food, fried rice and curry.'

The man is already salivating.

'Sit in the corner with your kid. Your good wife had better not keep us waiting.'

An hour later, Dad is taken by the officers to be interrogated. Meanwhile, I sit with my forehead on my knees, avoiding all eye contact. The men around me are agitated. I am aware that I am one person too many, and a Muslim at that. My father returns battered and broken. He gives me a sad but insistent look, as if he is trying to tell me something. The officer orders me to follow him. I try to reassure Dad with my eyes: *Yes Dad, I remember... we were taking a shortcut.*

I am terrified.

The interrogation takes place in a tiny room. I am surrounded by three men who shove and push me around between them as if I were a skittle struggling to stay upright.

'Why did you enter state-owned property?'

'We wanted to take a shortcut to the road.'

'You trespassed on government land, vermin!'

'I'm sorry, sir. I didn't think. I didn't know that I was doing anything wrong. We didn't want to harm your land.'

'Where were you going?'

'Home, sir.'

'Where were you coming from?'

'We had gone shopping at the market, sir.'

'What do you do?'

'I'm a student. I'm studying for the matriculation certificate.'

'A *kalar*, studying for the matriculation certificate? Do you take us for idiots? You utter moron!'

'Sir, with all due respect, I'm taking my exams next year.'

'Do you realise what danger you're in, you snotty little shit?'

'Yes, sir.'

'I see filthy *kalar* liars like you every day and I send them to prison for life.'

The interrogation continues in the same vein, with the usual humiliations and degrading violence so mortifying that it is hard to put into words.

Back in the cell I find the Rakhine licking the last grains of rice from his fingers. Mum has been. My father says to me quietly, 'Mum is going to collect money from the family and the community. It's our last chance.'

The night is interminable. Dad is taken away several times. Despite the beatings, he sticks to the original story that I have confirmed. Meanwhile, I'm subjected to the grumbling and muttering of my cellmates, and the boss is expecting other titbits from us. On the outside, Mum is trying her hardest to raise the huge sum of money demanded by the authorities for our freedom. Friends and family all chip in. Once the police have the enormous wad of kyats in their hands, they finally decide that we are innocent and release us. The worst has been avoided. If we had been transferred to the national prison, it would have been impossible to buy our freedom, and we would have spent the rest of our days in the cells, awaiting death.

We walk home, crushed by this terrifying night. Dad says nothing. At Granny's hut, big basins of water from the well are ready and waiting. We have a long wash in the backyard before lying down on the bamboo floor in the main room. Mum brings us something to eat to help restore our strength. Nojum and Rohima fan us. Once we have rested, Dad gathers us all together.

'Children, you are all outlaws here just because you exist. You can't do anything about that, and neither can your mother or I. Even if we use the law to claim what we are legally entitled to, we will always lose. If you are arrested, your only guarantee of survival is firstly to never admit that you are a Rohingya and secondly to bribe the authorities as quickly as you can, even if you end up owing money to your friends.'

Dad wants us to understand that the law will never protect us. In other countries, the police maintain order and keep citizens safe, here they just bleed people dry. Only money can bring us justice.

'Habib and I managed to secure our release today because our friends helped us. They know that we will be there to help them if they have a problem. Always be there when someone needs you. It is a sacrifice at the time, but it will save your life one day.'

22

Routine

I throw myself into my studies with greater zeal than ever, spending all my free time and energy revising. Following the recent student demonstrations, the universities have been closed until further notice. As 1997 gets underway, I hear in the school corridors that the only courses still open are the ones at the GTI[†], originally intended for the children of civil servants. They offer recognised electrical engineering apprenticeships. My classmates talk about this as the only possible way of continuing their studies. The idea germinates in my brain and I start thinking about it seriously.

I rise at dawn, gulp down a cup of tea, and jump on my bike. I cycle past three soldiers posted at the huge building site where the Lawkananda pagoda is being erected. They are guarding twenty Rohingya carrying sacks of cement and stones. I can feel the blood rushing to my head, and pedal on as fast as

---

† Government Technical Institutes.

I can. Will this country never let us live in peace? Will I have to fear for my life at every turn? All the hours that we give to their army and the construction of their religious buildings, all the financial contributions that we make. These starving workers are toiling to build one of the most lavish Buddhist monuments in Sittwe. I cannot help thinking that this edifice adorned with hundreds of kilos of gold leaf is just a fraud built on the back of our people's enslavement.

Tensions mount for the second time this year. Our village is surrounded. Many Rohingya are beaten. Rakhines vandalise our mosques and homes. We have no choice but to defend ourselves. A number of villagers are arrested. Fear of these arbitrary attacks and arrests spreads. We can no longer obtain permission to leave the village except when we are forcibly requisitioned to build roads, military camps, or houses for Buddhist settlers. We are confined to our neighbourhoods, and the additional restrictions make it increasingly difficult for many of us to trade and earn a living. Those who possess some kind of identity document and attempt to leave their villages for a few days to travel a short distance to visit loved ones are interrogated, harassed, threatened, and end up having to bribe the police.

I remain cautious and go out as little as possible.

23

The young woman

I like to pass the time of day with the older members of our community who sometimes sit on the little bench behind our hut. Hla Aung, a lawyer who has just been released from prison, and other friends of my dad's come to chat with him and exchange views over a cup of black tea. I learn a lot from spending time with them. I am fascinated by how calm they are. Their memories are like an open book in which I learn the other history of Arakan, our region. The history that cannot speak its name, the secret history of which they are among the few guardians.

At school, our teachers often make reference to the Bengalis who supposedly invaded Arakan and were butchered in their thousands by the great and worthy Rakhine warriors defending their kingdom. This is the story that is recounted in the new textbooks and much discussed in the school corridors.

Dad is constantly writing in his old yellowing notebooks. He says that our history of Arakan and our identity will only be known through written documents. Some Rohingya intellectuals confide in him that they too keep their precious memories carefully hidden under a mattress or a wooden floorboard, sometimes along with old photos from the 1930s. These snaps of young educated Rohingya lawyers, doctors, and teachers are rare, and date from a period that was very different from the brutal apartheid under which we now live.

At times when the general atmosphere is calmer than usual in my Muslim neighbourhood, or when we are surrounded by soldiers during states of emergency and all we can do is sit it out, waiting for the end of the siege, I spend hours listening to these veterans. They tell the story of the Rohingya, what makes us different, our culture, our achievements, our hardships, and our heroes. I become increasingly aware of our cause, our present condition, and our past riches.

I've got my nose buried in my physics books when Dad enters the house accompanied by Mr Nuramad, my English language teacher from the school. He is the same age as my father and one of the wealthiest men in the neighbourhood. He belongs to the Kaman ethnic group, Muslims who are better regarded than us. Kaman means 'archer'. The elders say that the Kamans arrived here from India in the sixteenth century as archers to defend Arakan.

My father speaks first: 'Habib, I've told Mr Nuramad a lot about you and your excellent school results. He would like to speak to you.'

The man smiles and invites me to sit down next to him.

'My boy, I have something to ask you. Your teachers are full of praise for you. You are very gifted at school and you work hard. My close friend's daughter, Nway Nway is struggling to keep up in class, particularly in science. Would you be prepared to spend a few hours a week helping her with her schoolwork?'

I am unable to hide my embarrassment, tinged with huge pride that this highly respected man, known for his generosity and open-mindedness, has noticed me and made this unexpected request. This kind of proposal is unusual in our communities where a woman spending time alone with a man is generally regarded with suspicion. Nway Nway and I have often crossed paths on the way to and from school, but I have never talked to her, although I am certainly not oblivious to her disconcerting grace and beauty.

I realise that even though this is probably going to disrupt my own schedule, we all have to work together, and that this is an honour and recognition which cannot be refused. From now on, I will go to Nway Nway's house every other day to help her with her schoolwork.

Nway Nway turns out to be very pleasant and enthusiastic. From the very first lesson, she waits for me on the doorstep. She watches me carefully and seems to be taking on board what I'm saying, but as soon as my explanations become a bit complicated she is distracted. Her mind often wanders and she is unable or unwilling to follow my reasoning. Her casual gestures, shining eyes, and her way of running her hand through her long hair to tidy it up sometimes distracts me. I often reprimand her for her lack of concentration.

'I've just explained that, Nway Nway. You're not listening to me. I've asked you the same question several times and given you the answer. Why do you always get it wrong?'

Nway Nway stares at me with her big black eyes and smiles teasingly without saying a word. I am troubled.

'Listen, Nway Nway, I don't know what you're thinking about, but you're not paying attention. Try to concentrate on studying for your exam.'

'Do you think it is really that easy? I'm not as clever as you!' she replies insolently.

'It's a question of willpower. Make an effort. If you fail the matriculation certificate, both of us will have wasted our time. Our parents will be extremely disappointed and my teacher will lose faith in me.'

Over the course of these lessons, we grow fonder of one another. Nway Nway brings me little gifts, the perfect excuse for avoiding more scholarly talk. Sometimes it's a little parcel of fried rice, sometimes cassettes of Burmese love songs. She also likes to give me pretty cards and biscuits that she has baked herself. It is almost as if she is trying to get me to notice her more. After the lessons, she continually invents excuses to spend more time together.

'Will you take me to the market, Habib? Please, I need to buy some vegetables for Mum and I am worried that I won't be able to carry them all on my own.'

I have great respect for her family and am incapable of refusing her anything. Nevertheless, I know that I mustn't overstep the mark. She sits on the back of my bicycle and I keep my fingers crossed that we won't bump into any soldiers or Rakhine ultra-nationalists who will humiliate me.

While I'm reciting my lessons, the thought of her soft jet-black hair suddenly drifts into my mind. I try to rid myself of the image. It is impossible for me to fall in love. I must concentrate on my goals and my studies. I must succeed. But the more I try to be cold and objective with Nway Nway, the more attention she lavishes on me.

I ignore all her hints, and reprimand her sharply several times. I am sure that I'm not in love with her, but love and the meaning of love are issues that I spend more and more time thinking about. I borrow a book from a friend written by a Burmese author about life. I memorise this quote: 'Marrying at a young age generally brings much uncertainty over the years. Such a union prevents the man and the woman from having their own experiences and their own appreciation of life and future responsibilities.'

I feel that I need to build my own life before becoming involved in a relationship. The contact with Nway Nway has exposed me to new feelings, and I know that carefree and magical moments will one day exist for me, but for now I firmly believe that love will only bring misfortune and disappointment to a Rohingya student in Arakan. Falling in love would be an irreversible error. All around me I see promising students spending too much time on their relationships, writing love songs and serenades to the girls they love, and dropping out of school. I sense this danger when I am with Nway Nway. Love between two teenagers can turn into devastating grief in just a matter of weeks. Strong passions can have a dramatic effect in an environment like ours, which is so compartmentalised by tradition and caste.

Being in love is even worse for Rohingya because, besides parental approval, we need state permission to get married, which most of us cannot afford and is often impossible in any case. In Buthidaung and Maungdaw, Rohingya are systematically forbidden to marry.

This is why I don't want to become involved in a relationship. For me, love can only lead to failure. Becoming a lawyer is the only thing I want to think about. I have set my mind on this one objective.

At night, I carry on listening secretly to the BBC and Voice of America with Dad, and I gradually start to realise that we are living in one of the worst dictatorships on the planet. Is the international community aware that we exist in this state of apartheid in the depths of a country cut off from the rest of the world? Do Burmese people from other states know who we are? These radio programmes raise all kinds of questions in my mind and provide material for lengthy whispered discussions with Dad that never shake his faith in union: 'Ethnic groups and different political, ethnic, and religious ideologies must one day unite to defeat the dictatorship. It is an enormous challenge because disunity is one of this military junta's great battlegrounds.'

This evening, once again, the army has placed our neighbourhood under close surveillance. No one is authorised to leave their zone. A curfew is in place between 8 pm and 6 am. I am unable to go to school during the three-day blockade. Soldiers are stationed at all the entry and exit points in the district. Gatherings of more than two people, besides family, are forbidden. The central water pump is cut off, along with several telephone lines in the village. Mum has enough dried-fish provisions for us to hold out for four days. Our neighbours, however, are starving. Mutual aid is more vital than ever.

To kill time, I read the few out-of-date foreign magazines that are lying around. They transport me far away from Sittwe, the military threat, and the daily racism. This is my escape and, through the accounts that I read, I discover the emotions and feelings of men and women who live elsewhere, places where difference is celebrated, bringing people together rather than pitting them against one another. But I also read stories of love made impossible due to class inequality. I recognise my own emotions and feelings in these articles. So near and yet so far from all these other peoples around the world. My reading takes me on new adventures, and fills me with excitement and enthusiasm, but also makes me wary. I imagine other lifestyles, other ethnic groups, other countries. I dream, intrigued by an outside world with no apartheid, no soldiers at every street corner, no spies or informers. My voracious reading helps me to understand the challenges faced by other cultures, by each different generation, and by all peoples.

24

Thwarting apartheid

1997

In Africa, there is a country where white people live separately from black people. Black people do not have the right to vote and are forbidden to have sexual relationships with white people. The different communities are segregated in order to protect the power of the whites. Apartheid exists there too. Well, it did. They abolished it a few years ago.

In northern Arakan, a similar, but nameless, system exists: the segregation of *kalars*, non-citizens since the law passed by the ex-dictator Ne Win, which has been blithely maintained by his successor Than Shwe. The NaSaKa continue to terrorise the towns in which we are confined. Settlers' villages, known as NaTaLa, are springing up like mushrooms on land confiscated from the Rohingya. Arakan must become Burmese and Buddhist. That is our version of apartheid.

When I see the results table, I feel immensely proud. The

Burmese name that I use for school appears on the list of students who have passed the exam. I have succeeded, and Dad will be proud of me too. It is a major triumph over what seemed a certain destiny. Although I will not be able to collect my certificate, because I have no identity documents, at least the results are there and accessible to educational establishments across the country. But the universities in Sittwe, the only ones in which I could have enrolled, remain closed. I am not allowed into any state other than Arakan, and cannot travel outside Sittwe. I feel a growing need to put my knowledge into practice, to use my brain to serve my community. I want to have some control over my destiny. I don't want it to end here.

Dad has faith. He still dreams of his children becoming lawyers. I want to believe in that too. One thing is certain: there is no future for me in Sittwe. All I can hope for here is a hand-to-mouth existence as an odd-job man or, at best, an advisor for Rohingya at the hostel. Another option would be to work as a market trader with my parents and Granny.

I decide to leave and try my luck in Maungdaw in the North where many Rohingya live and a handful of international humanitarian organisations have obtained authorisation to set up offices, so I might be able to meet foreign volunteers and doctors. I don't know exactly what I am looking for, but my instinct tells me to go. My excellent school results might open doors where everything seems totally barred to me. I save as much money as I can to be able to leave Sittwe as soon as possible. My parents and uncles also help me out financially. I'm finally ready to approach the 11 Burmese district authorities. Systematic corruption raises the barriers of racism even higher. Military intelligence, the police, and the village Peace and Development Council all take their share of the savings that I have put aside.

I have also managed to assemble all the letters of recommendation that I need to present to the immigration service, my final port of call. Now that we are foreigners in our own country, this is where we have to report. The officer takes my money and the dispensation documents. He stamps them, and casually throws a piece of paper on the desk without even looking at me. He gestures for me to leave.

I can feel my heart beating as I exit the building, clutching the piece of paper that gives me my independence, the document that I hope will open doors for me.

'Form 4. Suspect individual. Temporary travel permit. Fourteen days maximum.'

Fourteen days to build my dream. Fourteen days to change my destiny.

Dad hides neither his respect nor his apprehension as he gives me his final words of advice before I leave.

'Be careful, Habib. The Rohingya are in the majority there, but Maungdaw is a prison-town where they are gradually trying to concentrate us together so that they can control us more effectively. It will be easier to enter Maungdaw than to leave it. Be smart and keep your eyes peeled. As soon as you arrive, go and see the elders. They will explain how to avoid the traps. Then do your best to approach the NGOs. If you don't manage to make contact, you should leave as quickly as possible before you get stuck there. You will be more of an outlaw there than you are here. Their prisons are places where Rohingya are left to die. Please be extremely careful.'

At the crack of dawn, I join the queue of Rohingya waiting next to the boat while the Rakhine passengers embark and take their seats. The police order us to sit on the ground while they collect the special taxes payable by the 'Bengalis'. A departure stamp costs five hundred kyats. We board, and around 20 of us cram in next to the engines which are already spewing out thick brown smoke. The boat is ready to depart. Three officers gesture to the skipper to wait. They come on board and head towards us.

'*Kalars*, you are on a jetty that we built for Buddhists. Blacks have to pay a land-use tax of three hundred kyats.'

I think about it. Have I ever heard of this particular levy in the long list of taxes that my family has had to pay in Sittwe? Probably yes, but most likely presented in some other way, under a different name.

None of us dares to answer back. We hope to avoid this kind of harassment and spontaneous racketeering, but it is fairly standard practice and comes as no surprise to any of us. No Rohingya lacks the basic savvy to board a boat without a wad of banknotes to pay the craziest taxes that they can invent. The authorities certainly do not lack imagination.

Our boat takes five hours to reach Buthidaung. Once alongside the jetty, we have to surrender once again to the special treatment for Rohingya. We are required to pay 250 kyats for a stamp. Then an officer makes us pile into a truck that takes us along a narrow and perilous road to Maungdaw. The vehicle is stopped three times during the 15-mile journey to our final destination. We are searched, shoved around, questioned, and money is extorted from us.

I finally make it to Maungdaw. Rohingya hurriedly come and go. Among the many overt signs of poverty are women in shabby shawls that fail to conceal their leathery skin and emaciated bodies, naked children covered in scabs, bellies swollen by malnutrition, who sit on the filthy ground playing with bits of string, and men dragging heavy carts that are normally drawn by oxen. A few squashes and mangoes for sale at the roadside constitute an entire family's hopes of surviving another day. The sheer number of people in the town is unbelievable. I have never seen so many Muslims, nor have I ever seen so much sadness and pain in people's eyes. I find the house where the family of one of my friends in Sittwe lives. Their poverty has not got the better of their generosity, and they take me in willingly. The mother offers me a bowl of hot broth while the father explains to me how the town works.

'It's hard to imagine getting out of Maungdaw. The town is surrounded by Burmese army regiments. There is no hospital and very few resources here. The junta's hidden agenda is to concentrate the Rohingya population in towns close to the borders where they are left to die. Every day is a struggle to find enough food and drinking water, a battle to stay alive. Many of our young people are regularly taken away and arrested. We have a few hens and two goats, but the NaSaKa controls everything. If a goat gives birth, we are heavily taxed. If one of us happens to lose his way or is delayed by an incident somewhere and misses the roll call on just one evening, he is struck off the household list and can only return home by paying for the privilege.'

Despite the hardships of life in Maungdaw, I have to act fast and find a job. There is no time to lose. I only have 14 days.

NaSaKa trucks continually patrol the streets. The very word 'NaSaKa' visibly strikes terror into the locals. Barely five years after it was established, the crimes that it has committed already populate nightmares in Maungdaw. The NaSaKa rapes, kills, humiliates, beats, steals, and loots. I am stopped and checked several times by NaSaKa officers, and they take me away on various occasions for two, three, and four-hour stretches. Each time, the outcome is uncertain, and I feel like I am staring into the jaws of hell. To escape their clutches, I relinquish my watch, a small radio, and some money. Meanwhile, I approach the international humanitarian organisations, hoping to persuade them to give me a job. I quickly realise that I am not the only Rohingya looking for work. On day six, I manage to arrange an appointment with a manager, but he is only available to meet me two weeks later. My visa is due to expire in eight days, but I can't afford to let this opportunity pass.

Every night, it's the same story: I'm scared to go to sleep for fear of being taken away by the NaSaKa who I sense are stalking their prey and circling ever closer.

My visa expires. I am still in Maungdaw. Anonymous, invisible, but hunted all the same. I can no longer leave the town without authorisation, nor can I stay without valid papers. I decide to tackle the problem head on by approaching the district leader. I purchase a letter of recommendation from him so that I can apply to become a resident of Maungdaw.

The day of my appointment at the offices of the major international organisation finally arrives. My heart is beating fast, full of hope.

Once there, my illusions are quickly shattered. I find myself at the end of a long line of hundreds of candidates. When my turn finally comes, the interview is conducted in haste. The official offers me work for a few days as a street sweeper. So I approach another organisation. The manager agrees to see me and explains that he is the only person who can recommend me to head office for a job. After several appointments with no progress on my application, my host family gently hint that I won't get a job unless I bribe the recruiter. It is standard practice, but I don't have enough money left. I'm gutted.

Three months go by and I survive on odd jobs here and there while my savings are gobbled up by letters of recommendation, permits, and arbitrary taxes. In the end, I am forced to face facts — I can't settle in Maungdaw. The obstacles are greater than in Sittwe. Rohingya are more oppressed here than anywhere else. I need to return to Sittwe, but the prospect of dealing with local government officials terrifies me. If they find out that my permit is no longer valid, I'll be arrested, tortured, and imprisoned. I will never see my family again.

Fifty thousand kyats borrowed from a distant cousin of my mother is enough to bribe the necessary officials and obtain a temporary travel permit. There are even more checks on the return journey to Sittwe than the outward one, but I arrive in my village safe and sound.

I sense my parents' relief when they see me coming through the door. Having me back alive is already an achievement in their eyes. Despite my plans not working out as I had hoped, I cannot let myself give up. Since the university closures in 1992, the GTIs have become very popular with students who have matriculation certificates. I know that I am forbidden to leave Arakan, but I am curious to find out whether by hiding my ethnic origin I would be accepted by one of the schools. So I send my results in my Burmese name to a few GTIs across Myanmar. No one can arrest me for just applying.

The weeks go by. I work with my father at the market. We sell fish that we either breed ourselves or buy from fishermen. In my free time, I listen to songs, read articles and old books, and listen to the radio as usual, all in English, and all clandestinely because consuming foreign cultural goods is a crime.

One evening, Dad hands me a letter. I have been accepted on an electrical engineering course in Shan State. The school hasn't found out that I am a Rohingya. My father says nothing but looks deeply troubled. I sense that it is hard for him to stop me taking risks elsewhere, as our life in Sittwe is already a minefield.

What I want more than anything else is to be able to study. I am prepared to face danger to achieve my dreams.

25

Love and flight

A friend stops off at my house.

'Here, Habib, this is for you, from Nway Nway.'

I take the sheet of paper that he hands me and find a quiet corner in the backyard.

You're the one that I've chosen, Habib. Please think about what we have in common. Don't let your personal desires and dreams destroy what we could have between us.

I tremble as I read her love note. For an instant, I recall her delicate hands caressing the words and sentences in her exercise book as I read and explained the lessons to her. Nway Nway — what does she know about my dreams?

I straddle my bike and cycle to my tree. The imminent turning point in my life occupies all my thoughts. *You have passed your exams, Nway Nway, a huge achievement for you and immense satisfaction for me. It would be better for both of us if I don't succumb to your charms. It would jeopardise everything and I would never find the courage to leave. I would end up staying here waiting to be trampled underfoot, humiliated, unable to progress in life, study, or gain any qualifications. What would be the point? What would I have given you? Disappointment.*

Love is just another obstacle that I don't want to inflict on myself as I try to escape my destiny.

But you, dear Nway Nway, you are not Rohingya, you are Kaman. All doors are open to you, your future should be about pursuing your studies as far away as possible, not getting married, not now.

I have other challenges to face before I can allow myself to love. I will not commit to a lifelong relationship as long as I continue to be deprived of peace and tranquillity. I cannot start a family without the prospect of having the freedom to enjoy the simple pleasures in life, and that will take time.

You're young, Nway Nway, and I am just a student. You'll quickly forget me and that is best for you.

I decide not to write back to her, I want her to forget me. I don't want to leave myself open to any possibility of a relationship.

Back in the house, I organise my few possessions, including my books and notebooks. This is all that will be left of me.

26

The big departure

This is goodbye, but I am the only one who knows. I don't want to look at them, or hug them and make them sad. Tomorrow, before dawn, I am leaving.

This evening I can't help shooing my sisters away when they start squabbling. I'm curt with my mother who continually asks me questions. I don't utter a single word to Babuli even though we usually giggle together all the time. I ignore my father. I shut myself away mentally in an attempt to alleviate the pain of departure.

I am going on a perilous journey to escape this bottomless quagmire of life as a Rohingya. If they knew what I was planning, they would try to dissuade me. I have to believe; all I need to do is believe despite all Dad's best advice. Tomorrow, I will leave without looking back, without saying goodbye to them. I will only come back if I can bring good news. Let me try to restore the hope and pride that has been stolen from us.

I am leaving, and I am well aware of the risks. If I am caught by the authorities, indefinite imprisonment or death await. I know this. But if I succeed, a world of possibilities is waiting to be discovered outside Arakan

Then you will be proud of your son, Dad.

It is seven o'clock in the morning. The room is filled with the fragrance of steaming tea. I gulp down some noodles and broth that Mum has made, put one shirt on over the other, slip into my flip-flops and take the wad of banknotes that Mum has agreed to give me without asking why. Does she suspect?

'I'm going into town,' I shout out.

Without waiting for anyone to reply, I head down the mud path towards the jetty. I catch sight of the puzzled look on Mum's face as she watches me disappear from view.

Goodbye, Mum. If only you knew how much I love you and Dad and all the others. I hope that you will understand.

There is a cargo ship in the port. I stand there for a long time, taking deep breaths and staring out to sea, as I watch the comings and goings. Men, foremen, and lots of labourers. I take a last deep breath before blending into the group with all the conviction I can muster. Sacks of rice are being stacked up, I grab one and throw it on my shoulder. I join the line of men who are loading the boat with provisions for the capital, Yangon.

I dump my load on board and return for another. Four, five, six, ten sacks of rice. I slip away to the rear of the boat and down into the hold. Time passes painfully slowly before the vessel finally gets underway.

The engines make the deck shudder. The ship sails away from these prison-lands, these hostage-lands. We leave Sittwe Delta behind us and head out to sea across the choppy waters of the Bay of Bengal. The horizon is huge, blue, and uncertain.

I need to keep myself constantly busy so that no one notices me. I go from one end of the ship to the other, making myself useful while staying invisible. Sometimes I'm a passenger, others I'm a crew member, depending on the perceived danger. I am constantly alert. The number of passengers and crew on such a big ship works in my favour and helps me to stay anonymous. I try to anticipate what might happen next, alternately scrubbing the deck, hauling on the ropes, and hiding between the sacks of rice in the hold. I quickly find my way around.

Hours and days pass. I suffer from seasickness and a gnawing pain in my stomach. The boat calls into various ports, and then finally my destination slides into view: Yangon†.

---

† Yangon, previously called Rangoon, was the capital of Myanmar until 2006.

27

My new identity

The port is crawling with police. I melt into the crowd of workers who are unloading the boat while the captain negotiates with the authorities. Calmly, I deposit the merchandise and make my way to a group of buildings behind the port. I roll under a hole in the fence, then zigzag through the streets to leave a false trail. I finally slow down. It is better to walk normally to avoid arousing suspicion. I hail a taxi that drops me in the centre of the Minghala district 20 minutes later. A few streets on, I find the place that I am looking for. A dilapidated apartment block, whose walls and stairwell are stained with betel-juice spit. I climb to the fifth floor, and knock. The door opens.

'I'm Habib, Begom's son.'

'Begom ... God protect my little sister! Quick, come in.'

Inside the apartment, five children are sitting on the living room floor. One of them is drawing shapes in an old exercise book, closely watched by the others. Ali, my auntie's husband, clasps my hands in his.

'Tinie, go and fetch some tea and apples. What are you doing here, Habib?'

'I don't want to put you to any trouble. I've fled Arakan.'

'How did you end up here? Did anyone see you come in?'

'No, don't worry, uncle.'

'I can't keep you here. Stay tonight, but tomorrow you'll have to leave. The neighbours don't like us living here. If the authorities find you here, we will all be arrested and imprisoned. Since we left Arakan, we have told everyone that we are from a Muslim ethnic group in Shan State. If they find out that we are Rohingya, that's the end of us.'

He pauses and looks uneasy before continuing, 'What are you going to do in Yangon?'

'I'm not planning to stay here. I want to go to Irrawaddy to continue my studies.'

'May God help you achieve the impossible, Habib. Don't ever tell anyone that you come from Arakan. From today, you're a Muslim from Shan State like us. Tomorrow, you must leave this apartment, and for everyone's safety, don't try to contact us again unless there's no other option.'

My auntie has cooked a big dish of rice with dried fish and curry. But the atmosphere is tense. Denunciations are commonplace in Yangon, where the general feeling is that all Rohingya must disappear. Ali and his family live every day in fear of their secret being discovered.

The next day, I leave as planned. My uncle gives me 50,000 kyats, enough to pay the taxes and bribes as I continue my journey. He also gives me the address of a place where I can have a false identity card made that will help me to avoid arrest and pass roadside checkpoints.

'While you're in Yangon, stay in the area around Insein Bazaar. You're more likely to go unnoticed there,' he advises me before I leave.

After taking the photos for my identity card, I head to the address that Ali gave me. It is an electronic goods shop, and I don't need to introduce myself. The old shopkeeper knows as soon as he sees me.

'You're after papers, aren't you?'

'Yes, sir.'

He looks me up and down with a frown and says, 'I'll help you, son.'

He gestures to an adolescent who works with him to escort me. We go down a few streets and into an insalubrious building much like all the others. The young man tells me to wait and returns a couple of minutes later.

'It's okay, you can go up.'

The gates open. A man in the entrance looks at me and turns to the young lad who brought me here. 'Is that him?'

The adolescent nods. We climb the stairs to a gloomy apartment on the top floor.

'It's for an identity card. Muslim from Shan State.'

I'm told to sit down, confirm the details, and pay.

'Come back in three days. Your ID will be ready.'

I manage to phone Dad via the district operator in Sittwe. I have to be brief because people might be listening. Perhaps they are already looking for me, and I can't risk making my father an accomplice. Especially not now, when I've only just escaped.

'Dad? I'm in Yangon. Don't worry about me. I'm doing what I have to do.'

'They came to question me. You're not on the list anymore.'

These are the only details he gives. But I know what it means — arrest, interrogation, torture, another tax. And my name struck off the list of people living in my grandmother's house. There is no going back. I have to succeed, I have no home now. If things don't work out as I hope, I won't be able to go back unless, at best, I pay an exorbitant tax and, at worst ... I don't even want to think about it.

I'm now an outlaw everywhere in my country and I have a daunting task ahead of me. If I want to live free outside Arakan, my prison-region, I need to be reborn with my new Burmese identity. My only allies from now on will be my education, and money.

I go to the Insein district as my uncle advised. I wander the streets for a few hours, familiarising myself with the area and hiding in the crowd of betel sellers and people from many different ethnic groups. I try to quell my fear and appear at ease in this new environment that seems totally indifferent to my presence. I must not attract anyone's animosity.

A terrifying prison stands in the centre of the district, the kind that once you enter you never leave, or if you do it's when you're old and sick. I remember the stories of innocent men and women who were imprisoned there and emerged battered and broken, to be taken in again by their families in Sittwe. None of them were political prisoners or criminals, just men and women who were the wrong colour, the wrong religion. They were people like Mum's cousins, imprisoned for many long and hellish years, from which they emerged utterly traumatised.

The market is swarming with people selling vegetables, thanaka, fabric, and traditional medicinal plants.

A dark-skinned Burmese man, with his beard dyed orange and a kindly appearance, calls out to me from his sandal stall: 'What brings you here, brother? Want to buy some flip-flops?'

'No, but I can help you sell them.'

'Sit down, let's talk about it. You look like a good lad. Call me Aung Nyi.

Aung Nyi rolls a piece of areca nut in a betel leaf covered in slaked lime and ground clove and holds it out to me. In the middle of the crowd of people strolling around, we chew this inexpensive traditional *quid* that suppresses the appetite and provides a little energy boost. We start talking about the popularity of velvet flip-flops, which he says sell better than the others. He senses that my mind is elsewhere and that I am finding my bearings in the town. He gives me a few tips. From the way he speaks, I suspect that he is a Rohingya. We share the same wound. But what Muslim in Yangon or elsewhere would tell a complete stranger that he is a Rohingya? The word that dare not speak its name ...

'You should try the shop over there. They need an odd-job man.'

I thank him and walk over to the shop in question. It turns out that they do need someone, and they agree to employ me on daily wages to repair air-conditioning units and fridges. The job becomes a perfect hiding place and gives me enough to eat and save a few kyats.

I sleep here, there, and everywhere, hiding under cardboard boxes, down dark alleyways, and between wooden packing cases. I even spend the night in a corridor at my workplace. I make every effort to avoid being spotted by informers and by the authorities patrolling the streets. The vans transporting new prisoners appear with frightening regularity. I catch glimpses of people gazing hopelessly into the distance out of the navy-blue bars. The last sight that they will have of the land of the living.

My ID card is finally ready.

I take a seat in the back of an old bus heading for Irrawaddy, several hundred miles north of Yangon. There are many checkpoints on the road. At one, where we stop late at night, I see rifles, and closed expressions on faces that betray no sign of humanity. These are soldiers with only one thing in mind. Perhaps they have suffered themselves and decided to turn torturer.

I hold out my new card.

'You're Muslim? Reason for travelling?'

'I'm visiting my uncle.'

'Stand to one side. We'll deal with you in a minute.'

I am taken aside with three other people, a Chin and two Muslims.

One of the soldiers pulls me brutally by the arm and shoves me into the cabin that serves as their office. He grabs me by the neck and crushes my head on the table.

'Hey, *kalar*! You think you can just go from one state to the other, as if you lived here? Search him!'

Another soldier violently shoves me against the wooden boards and removes from my fabric bag the little plastic pouch in which I keep a small amount of my money.

'How much are you going to give me?'

'A thousand kyats.'

'Do you take me for an idiot? Five thousand, no less.'

The man counts the notes and ends up pocketing 6,000 kyats.

'Okay, scram.'

The engine of the bus is running. I grab the rail just in time to jump in and return to my seat. We still have a 12-hour journey ahead of us. Interminable periods of waiting at checkpoints. I am taxed and humiliated by soldiers on two other occasions. Ordinary violence, no surprises there.

The journey finally ends. I wait for all the other passengers to alight before approaching the driver to ask him where I can find a cheap hostel. He tells me to go to the hostel run by the Union Solidarity and Development Association, a no-frills establishment managed by a friendly boss who frequently employs people to help out around the place.

When I enter the dreary room that serves as a reception, the manager is leaning on the counter doing his accounts. He looks up with a questioning expression.

'What do you want?'

'Have you got a place where I can sleep? I'm a student. I'm about to start an electrical engineering course and I'm looking for somewhere to stay.'

'Yes, we have rooms. What's your budget?'

'The minimum possible. In exchange, I can help you keep the hostel clean and welcome customers.'

'Come through to the rear courtyard, I'll show you where you can sleep. You can start by cleaning the toilets, they need a good scrub.'

I agree to be the odd-job man. Anything, as long as I have somewhere to sleep. The place I've been given is spartan. It's a tiny space that looks like a converted storeroom, at the end of a corridor reddened by betel spit. A worn blanket full of holes and an old cushion blackened by time and my predecessors mean that I won't have to sleep directly on the ground. It's perfect. I wash my shirt and *longyi* before lying down and shutting my eyes. I've made it this far. My first victory.

By the time I wake up, my clothes have had time to dry. They are spotless. I iron out the creases with the palm of my hand and splash some water over my face and body from a bucket left in the courtyard by the hostel manager.

I stand outside the training centre for a while, staring at it. I've dreamt about this moment for so long.

I'm trembling as I hand my admission letter to the head of school. He inspects it carefully. I can feel the heat rising in my cheeks and I find myself blushing. My hands are shaking so much that I am forced to hide them behind my back. I try to analyse his reaction while I remain bolt upright with a smile on my face, trying to look presentable. He knows where I come from now. He could react well or badly, that's the risk I'm taking.

'You're Muslim. That makes things very difficult. I understand your situation and realise that you achieved very good results in your final exams. Congratulations.'

My heart feels as if it is about to burst out of my chest. He looks at me for what seems an endless moment.

'Do you have money?'

'A little. I can find some. I'll need to work at weekends. I could also pay in instalments or borrow money.'

'Listen, it is impossible to enrol students in higher education without a valid identity card, and it is even more complicated for Muslims. You need a Burmese Buddhist guarantor to confirm your enrolment. I have a friend who can help you. You'll have to pay him two hundred thousand kyats to write a letter of recommendation for you. Once we have that, we can accept you on the course with the other students and you will be able to attend the same classes.'

I have less than 40,000 kyats. The Bamar to whom I have to pay the money agrees to give me a few months to raise the necessary funds. Alongside my classes and my work at the hostel, I'll have to find a weekend job.

By talking to the Muslims toiling away at the market, I learn how things work in Irrawaddy and manage to find a job in a household appliance repair shop.

My day begins at around five o'clock in the morning. I clean the hostel before heading to college with no breakfast. When I have enough energy, I read at night. I read everything that I can lay my hands on, as long as I am learning new ideas.

I spend a few kyats on a public telephone and manage to call my father. Before he hangs up, he gives me a final word of advice: 'You are intelligent. Work hard and one day you'll be able to find a proper job and support your elderly parents. Be brave, my son.'

I swallow a few mouthfuls of black tea left out on the low tables in the teahouse in the courtyard. Classes began two weeks ago. The other students scrutinise me.

I nod a greeting to a man sitting near me who seems to be a regular around here. I've heard the other students talking about him. With his grey hair, big intellectual glasses, and a calm expression on his round face, he is a man who commands respect. Unexpectedly, he comes over and sits next to me, pours himself a small cup of tea, and then refills my cup.

'I'm U Zaw Kyaw. I am a teacher here.'

'I'm Aung Soe Naing. You can call me Nyi Nyi. I am new here.'

From now on, I use my Burmese name, Aung Soe Naing, Nyi Nyi to my friends. Although that cannot hide the colour of my skin, it does mean that I go unnoticed on the papers that are passed between the school and the authorities.

'Which course are you taking here?'

'Electrical engineering.'

'Have you been here long?'

'Just a few days.'

'Where are you from?'

I hesitate before answering. He is a teacher, he seems friendly, and now that I am at the school and enrolled thanks to an admission letter sent from my home address, he can find out if he wants to. I decide to trust him.

'I'm from Arakan.'

His eyes suddenly light up. He smiles at me.

'It's unusual to meet someone like you in this province. We don't know much about Arakan here. It is one of the most complicated ethnic regions. I understand that it is quite hard for your people.'

I nod, totally incapable of saying any more as I am overcome with emotion. His words bring flashbacks from my past.

We sit in silence for a long time feeling Arakan's pain.

'If you need any information about the town or the school, I'd be happy to help.'

U Zaw Kyaw stands up and leaves, but over time we fall into the habit of meeting in the teahouse every morning to drink a cup of black tea and continue our conversation. We talk about the classes, his students, and his profession. He casually asks me many questions about my attitude to life and human relationships. I sense that he is testing me. I'm not sure I really understand, is he a spy? Or is he just trying to find out if he can trust me?

He finally opens up a bit.

'I used to be a member of the NLD†, Aung San Suu Kyi's opposition party, and I was arrested and imprisoned for several

---

† The National League for Democracy.

years because of it. I still work for the party, but clandestinely, because when I was released from prison, I signed a declaration to the effect that I would no longer be involved in politics.'

This revelation could put him in danger, but what it does most of all is to bring us closer and give me the freedom to confide in him. He talks to me about himself, his culture, his Buddhist religion, his classes, his education in the 1970s, and the NLD. We exchange opinions, and after a while we broach the subject of ethnic minorities and their rights. We talk about the country, and about poverty in Arakan.

He reminds me of my father, whom I miss a great deal. His gentleness and his ability to listen push me to think about my opinions in greater depth. Then suddenly, the taboo subject is raised.

'You've never said, but you're Muslim, aren't you?'

The blood rises to my cheeks. He knows that I am from Arakan. If I admit that I'm Muslim, he will know that I came here illegally and am probably a Rohingya. Nevertheless, I decide to play the honesty card. He is the only person since I left my family who has made any effort to really get to know me and understand my life, and he has shown real generosity.

'I don't want to make you feel uncomfortable. I am just curious. How did you manage to get admitted to the school, and then obtain the papers to travel outside Arakan? I have always thought that Muslims could not leave the state. You are the first one that I have met.'

There is no going back now. He already knows too much. So I explain to him about passing my exams and the impossibility of travelling. I tell him about my secret life and false papers.

'Professor, you know, I come from an ethnic group whose name I am not allowed to say.'

As I finish the sentence, I feel myself blushing again. If Dad could hear me, he would be furious that I am being so naive. I have said too much to this man. There are spies everywhere. How can I know if his revelations are just a tactic to make me talk? And what happens if he turns his back on me now that he has found out that I am a Rohingya? My brain is scrambled.

He notices my confusion and encourages me to continue: 'Tell me.'

I look at the ground, and in little more than a whisper, I say, 'We are called Rohingya.'

His silence makes me look up. He has a serious look on his face. He is thinking. My lips are still trembling from having uttered the forbidden word. I want to continue but I have nothing more to say to him. The ball is in his court. The atmosphere has become heavy.

'The name is largely unknown. I have heard of it, as a bad thing of course. But I don't know any more about it. Don't be afraid, Nyi Nyi, this will stay between us. However, I am honoured to have made your acquaintance. And what about the other ethnic groups in the country, do you know them?'

'I have never had the chance to meet many of them apart from a few Bamars and Rakhines in my village, but relations are very strained. I grew up in Chin State where I had some Christian and animist friends.'

'We have dozens of ethnic groups in this country. It is what makes it so culturally rich, and they could be extremely powerful if they united and rose up against the government. The government realises this only too well and that is why it does everything it can to cultivate division.'

A few weeks after we first met, U Zaw Kyaw invites me to join him in a small new restaurant outside school. He leans towards me and whispers so as not to be heard by inquisitive ears.

'Would you like to take part in a study with me and a few other students?'

I am surprised by his request.

'Of course.'

'I am counting on your discretion.'

'Tell me more.'

'I have started a research project to make an inventory of the country's natural resources. Each student is responsible for one state in Myanmar. You could be in charge of Arakan. It would be an excellent opportunity for you. As you'll see, my students are very tolerant and friendly. Many of them come from minority groups. Would you like to join us?'

I am delighted. U Zaw Kyaw sees me as someone who can help him achieve this. He is inviting me to join a select team to carry out an important mission on a national scale. I manage a rather timid 'Yes', but deep down I am ecstatic.

28

The riches of the Rohingya

The teacher and I climb a narrow staircase encased in bare concrete walls. When we reach the first floor, U Zaw Kyaw slips his hand through a security grille and knocks several times on the door. The bolts are pushed back, and the face of a young girl with her cheeks decorated in thanaka paste appears. She recognises the teacher and hurriedly unlocks the door. In this secret room, a dozen young people are sitting on the ground holding notebooks. They all look at me with great curiosity. The teacher greets them and start speaking: 'I'd like to introduce you to my new recruit. Nyi Nyi comes from Arakan and he's going to help us cover that region. We are all from different cultures and religions, but what brings us together in this project is our country and the army's plundering of all our resources. We need to give the Burmese people confidence again so that they realise that they are not as poor as the economic situation would suggest. They need to realise that in their gardens and forests, there is wealth, and that this wealth is being stolen from them by the junta. Without these resources, the army would not have the means to oppress us.'

Three students come up to me and carefully explain our work and our main areas of research. Our job is to make a meticulously detailed and accurate inventory of the natural resources in each of our regions. We need to focus on productivity, import, export, spending, and profits. The main resources covered by our research are petrol, gas, precious gems, wood, teak in particular, as well as agricultural produce such as rice, fish, sugar, and products that are exported, such as paper. We also need to make an inventory of mills and factories. I am soon infected by the enthusiasm and convictions of my research companions. Once we have a complete, well-informed report, it will be widely distributed. This is not a political action, it is educational and informative. Its sole aim is to open people's eyes, and raise awareness among the Burmese people and all the country's ethnic groups. They need to know. The reports that we are compiling grow thicker by the minute. Once they are ready, the truth will finally be revealed.

I get to know the other students in the group one by one. Tin, Aye Thein, Lulu, and Nay Win all welcome me freely and with no ulterior motive. I appreciate the kindness, tolerance, and open-mindedness of the group. This is something completely new to me, solidarity above and beyond difference. They are all very committed to the task, and no one calls me *kalar*. They call me by my first name, and I do the same with them. Apart from the teacher and two Bamar students, all of them come from ethnic minorities: Kachin, Chin, Mon, Shan, and Karen. We are all equals here, colleagues as well as friends.

Once the excitement of the first months wears off, I realise that although our work is completely harmless, justified, and legitimate, disseminating the results will not be without risk.

I share my fears with the others. The choice of people to participate in this research is vital. No information must be allowed to leak out. We need to think about how we are going to make this information public so that the truth will finally be known.

29

United

The weeks and months go by. The school, the teahouse, and empty classrooms have become our secret debate chambers. We meet up and discuss each other's progress. Our teacher U Zaw Kyaw recommends that we keep to groups of two or three students maximum and advises us to change the times and locations of our meetings to avoid being caught. The project broadens in scope and our pride at being involved feeds our enthusiasm. The feeling that we are each representing our respective regions and getting involved for the good of the people excites us.

Besides the academic impact, this secret mission to create an inventory is a wonderful catalyst for strong and deep relationships between students totally devoid of racial prejudices. I am eternally grateful to our teacher for having included me in this exceptional group, where I discover a Myanmar very different from the one in which I have lived until now. I become open to the prospect of ethnic reconciliation.

The sheer diversity of our origins is what makes our work so precious to us. Between the 15 of us, we frequently take flight on imaginary journeys around Myanmar. Yangon, Mandalay, Pyay, Myitkyina, Putao, Tachilek, Mawlamyine, Sittwe, and many other places. We become each other's geography teachers. The conversation sometimes turns to our country's leaders and the absurd way that they govern us, acting on whim and superstition. We talk about the names of towns that have been changed or banknotes that disappear overnight, bankrupting most of the rural population. All it takes is an astrologist to make a crazy prediction for the generals to completely upend the whole organisation of the country. I think about the 1982 law that Dad told me about. What could possibly have been going on in the head of the tyrant for him to hate us that much? Was it racism? Fear of the other? Or was it something to do with astrology and black magic?

On other occasions, we go off on tangents about our dreams for the future, burst out laughing in a teahouse, stroll through the streets together looking at movie and advertising posters, moments that make me forget everything — the difficulties that I face every morning, evening, and weekend, my financial worries, racism, my family who are still living in fear, and the fragility of the present moment. The time comes when I have to leave my friends and return to my other reality, which is decidedly less idealistic and more mundane. Cleaning the hostel from top to bottom to pay for my accommodation, making sure that I leave enough time for my studies and homework and learning my lessons by heart while doing without food (although avoiding this if I can), sleeping very little, staying strong, and making sacrifices, all in the name of progress.

30

The pamphlets

The bell rings for the start of lessons. I spent the night collating information on timber and mineral resources in Arakan and am struggling to wake up. I hurry from the main courtyard to the Physics classroom. I spot our teacher reading a newspaper in his usual place in the teahouse. He winks at me and I greet him in return, eager to meet up with him again to show him the results of my research. I admire this rare thinker and extraordinary philosopher of ordinary things. He is my role model.

Not long after, U Zaw Kyaw gives us new instructions. It is May 1998 and we are moving on to the next stage of our mission: the initial publication of our results. The pamphlets will be printed in two days' time. We need to be ready to go at midnight on Thursday.

I read the final version of the slogan that will accompany the list of revelations on Myanmar's resources, riches that belong to its people: 'The nation is rich. Be aware of this. Be proud of this. We are not poor.'

U Zaw Kyaw puts each of us in charge of a particular district, identified by the craftspeople who live there.

'Nyi, Nyi, you'll do the weavers' and blacksmiths' district.'

Without waiting, I discreetly slip out of the room with my canvas bag containing more than two hundred pamphlets slung over my shoulder. I break out in hot and cold sweats, my facial muscles are tense, and I feel nauseous. I am excited, nervous, enthusiastic, and afraid. I choke because I am breathing too fast. I need to calm down and get a grip on myself. I know the risks — if the police, soldiers, or spies catch me with the pamphlets, it's all over for me, forever.

It is five o'clock in the afternoon. I walk around my allocated area to prepare for my nocturnal mission and for any unforeseen events that might occur. Women sit on the ground selling baskets of fruit and pots of *mohinga*†. Next to them, a man presses sugarcane to make juice, female weavers fiddle with their thread, and other women serve coconut soup from their roadside stalls on the pot-holed street. I try to imagine their reaction tomorrow when they find the pamphlets on the pavements. Will they be scared, will they rise up in revolt, or will it make them think and share the information?

The rays of the setting sun soften the colours of my surroundings. I continue exploring every nook and cranny of the scene of the crime that I am about to commit. I discreetly observe the comings and goings of the colourfully dressed, blissfully unaware crowd, trying to convince myself that all these people walking around during the day will be sleeping at night. I plan the distribution of the pamphlets. I'll put one on

---

† Popular dish of noodles with fish sauce.

this doorstep, and one in front of that gate, I'll definitely put one on this traffic island.

By the time I return to the hostel, it is already nine o'clock. I try to concentrate, sitting on my straw mattress, head between my knees. I'm thinking, is all this really too audacious? I try to reassure myself that everything will be okay, that I am doing this for my country, for my people.

The alarm clock goes off. Midnight on the dot. It's time. Somewhere in the other districts of Irrawaddy, my comrades must also be getting ready to creep stealthily out of their rooms. We are acting together, but separately. In our respective canvas bags, we have thousands of pamphlets to distribute. Just like me, the others must be emerging from the stairwells or courtyards of their hostels, hurrying along alleyways, and sticking close to the walls to avoid being spotted. The town's main boulevards are dark and empty, and it is a moonless night. The town belongs to the packs of dogs rooting through the rubbish left by locals. Anyone wandering the streets at night is the perfect suspect, a criminal. I am trying not to tremble as I battle to maintain my self-control, the darkness is playing games with me. I pull myself together, grab the pamphlets from my bag, and overcome my fear. Everything happens as if I am in a kind of trance. One by one, the pamphlets fly away, spin in the air, and land on the ground.

Together we are rich! 135 or 140 ethnic groups, what difference does it make? The regime grows fat on people's suffering. Read, open your eyes.

The pamphlets are planted around the town like seeds. I am hoping against hope that these little secret words whispered by our group of dreamers will arouse public attention. Soon, in the early hours of the morning, hundreds of men and women will be hurrying along these streets to the market. I speed up, panting, listening out for the slightest sound that might be drowned out by the noise of the rats scuttling in and out of the drains and the dogs that growl as I pass. I stop in a doorway to catch my breath before setting off again determinedly, treading softly, guided by some unstoppable force.

Once I have emptied my bag, I take a number of detours back to the hostel, glancing back several times to check that I am not being followed. I finally enter the hostel through the backyard and head for the cupboard that serves as my bedroom. It is four o'clock in the morning before I fall asleep.

We all avoid one another for the next few days. We must not take any risks for several weeks or do anything that might give us away.

31

Checkpoints

My studies at Irrawaddy campus and my involvement in the secret research work all cost money. I desperately need to earn more to put aside in case I am arrested or forced to pay an arbitrary tax. The holidays are finally here, and with them the possibility of leaving Irrawaddy and going further afield to find more lucrative work.

Mohammed, a Muslim trader from Yangon I meet in the hostel, explains his business to me: he buys consumer goods at the border and makes a profit by selling them at a higher price in the capital's markets. I immediately offer my services and he accepts. He decides to send me to a town on the border to buy some Chinese grocery products and shoes. With my false identity card in my pocket, I am ready for the assignment.

Our vehicle is stopped in Lashio, at the first checkpoint. Armed soldiers check all the passengers. I can't hide the colour of my skin. They insult me, make me step off the bus,

163

inspect my false identity card and my bags. They take a vicious pleasure in dragging this out, forcing me to apologise for the effrontery of being there and making me address them as if I were a subordinate and they the masters. I take some blows to the head, but manage to keep the necessary composure to avoid arousing their instinct for domination. I allow them the pleasure of humiliating me without giving them any reason to arrest me. I repeat that I am a Muslim from Shan State and I am going to see a sick relation, as I hold out the money that could just save my life. The soldiers pocket my offering without batting an eyelid.

'Scram!'

The same scene is repeated a few metres further on where other soldiers demand their share. My fellow passengers wait in the car as I haven't yet paid for the journey. We continue on our way. There are so many checkpoints that I feel like I am on a never-ending road to nowhere.

As we travel towards the capital, I ask receptionists in roadside hostels if I can share their rooms, thus halving the cost of the accommodation. I eat very little and only in the evening. I drink copious amounts of water to stay alert and ensure that I have at least something in my stomach.

My assignment to purchase goods at the border only leads to more bullying and harassment. The risks that I take on this journey as well as the numerous taxes that I have to pay because I am a Muslim mean that I arrive in Yangon a week later completely broke. It is a bitter failure. But instead of destroying me, the experience makes me stronger.

I decide to contact some family members whose addresses Mum and Dad gave me. As I feared, my cousins Nurel and Ismail, like my Uncle Ali, do not want me to stay with them.

They give me some money, and I sleep outdoors in various places on the streets, often near betel vendors with whom I always get along. Brothers in misfortune.

Traders in the small port of Latha township give me occasional work packaging, weighing, checking shipment papers, and loading and dispatching crates to Sittwe, which pays three per cent commission on each parcel. The port is swarming with packers and soldiers and I find it hard to pass unnoticed. The packers push, shove, and generally bully me, almost tripping me up on numerous occasions.

'This parcel belongs to this filthy *kalar*.'

'Big nose, bushy eyebrows, tiny prick!'

'It'd be better for all of us if you went back to where you come from, Bengali invader!'

'Give me some money if you don't want me to squeal on you.'

I try to ignore them as much as I can, but they carry on humiliating and baiting me. I concentrate on my parcels.

The authorities are finally informed of my presence. After checking my false identity papers, two soldiers push me into a corner.

'Unwrap everything, we want to search it.'

I am forced to unwrap every single parcel that I have spent almost an hour packaging. I'll never manage to get them sent in time. I have no choice but to obey their orders and suffer in silence. One of the soldiers grabs me by the arm and makes me sit at his feet.

'Don't move! Stay down there!'

He pretends to be writing down the details from my parcels but his boorishness soon gets the better of him.

'Tell me that you are a filthy *kalar* pig!'

Here we go again. This puerile vulgarity makes me feel sick. I repeat the words that he wants to hear. He celebrates with glee. His colleague shoves me with his foot and slaps me while he carries on writing the codes in his notebook.

'Now if you want your parcels back, you'll have to pay a tax or we will send you to prison.'

I pay them, and they go off.

I emerge from this nth altercation physically and emotionally drained. I wrap up the parcels again and complete the formalities for urgent shipping. A few weary, exasperated tears roll down my cheeks, mixing with the sweat of the final effort of the day. Despite all my attempts to get by, I have to accept the truth of the matter, which is that my skin colour and my religion make the task almost impossible. But I have no option other than to persevere. I try my luck in other places with other traders where I continue to be confronted with the stigma of my skin colour. I would like to be able to aspire to something other than cleaning toilets in hostels or repairing electrical parts, but it will be a long journey.

The holidays come to an end and they have been so chaotic and degrading that I refuse to take stock. I simply accept the financial help offered by my cousin Ismail that will ensure my safe return to Irrawaddy with a small amount of cash in hand.

32

The spy

Youth hostel in Irrawaddy,
7 pm on 19 December 1999

The distribution of the pamphlets goes extremely well. As a security measure, we let two weeks pass before seeing one another again.

This evening, we are celebrating our victory with some well-deserved colas and orange sodas. The teacher congratulates us and tells us that he is proud of what we have achieved. A dozen of us have gathered in our comrade Law Win's room at the end of a corridor in the hostel where half of our group rents rooms.

Suddenly, there is a banging at the door. We signal to one another to keep quiet. One knock followed by a second. A short silence, then three abrupt knocks. It's the code. Law Win draws the bolt back, two of our friends enter the room, greet everyone, and sit down quietly next to us. The evening can continue.

Our group is more united and motivated than ever. We are planning to broaden the scope of our work, but are very much aware that the authorities are on the lookout and that there are spies everywhere.

'Any traitors, put your hand up!'

A little irony never goes amiss.

I have spent a lot of time thinking about the issue of informers and I decide to share my opinion with the others.

'If I thought someone was a spy, I wouldn't avoid him, in fact I think I'd actually approach him without telling him that I knew what he was. I'd joke around and chat about this and that so he wouldn't think I suspected.'

'Have you ever seen a spy then?' asks U Thant, one of my classmates.

Aye Thein bursts out laughing. 'Are you kidding? They are everywhere.'

I add, 'There are spies in towns like Sittwe, Maungdaw, Buthidaung, and Rathedaung. Some of them are our own people, who do it out of necessity. They inform the authorities of everything that goes on in the district and are rewarded for it.'

'Yes, it's the same in Kachin State — we are always on our guard, even among friends. You never know who you can really trust.'

'We actually know very little about spies, yet we feel surrounded by them. It's a good tactic to dissuade us from saying anything against the government.'

'What's sad is that there are no real secrets in the ethnic regions. People are just looking for ways to survive, grow crops on their land, and make sure that they have food to eat. There are no conspiracies or political protests, just people trying to get by.'

Law Win offers us all a bowl of fried rice. Our conversation returns to lighter subjects. Two students pick up their guitars and start strumming a gentle melancholic melody. For the first time in a long while, I feel good, almost at home, surrounded by these people who have become my second family, my adoptive brothers and sisters.

Another noise interrupts our little party. Suddenly, the door is kicked down. U Thant's face crumples. I feel a powerful shock wave travel down my back, almost knocking me off balance. Someone punches me in the chest, I shriek with pain, other screams drown mine out. Objects come crashing down, arms and legs flail in all directions. Something cold and hard smashes into my arm. I barely have time to look up before a hand gripping a rifle is raised in the air and slammed down on my skull.

33

Waking up in hell

It is cold and dark when I wake up. I am in unbearable agony. Where am I? The darkness only accentuates my anxiety. Two bodies are lying next to me. Who are they? The concrete floor is damp and freezing cold. Bars. I struggle to organise my thoughts. Am I in a military camp? The police station? A tomb? I don't want to believe it; it's a nightmare. All that for this. Please let me wake up again on my mattress in the hostel. I moan, but only a tiny muted sound comes out. I close my eyes tightly and open them again. They sting. An opaque veil clouds my eyes as if shielding me from reality. Nevertheless, this icy hell is definitely real.

It would be preferable if I just stopped breathing and let myself die before the junta's monsters get hold of me. There is a drumming in my head, my flesh aches, and I feel nauseous. I huddle up against the wall, leaning on my shoulder, which makes me cry out in pain. Fear courses through my body.

I feel shooting pains in my stomach. Suddenly, I hear the sound of echoing voices and footsteps. Decisive, mechanical steps: soldiers.

I lose consciousness once, twice. I am out for a long time.

34

I must survive

I open my eyes, I am aching all over.

'They've really laid into you.'

Around me I see grey walls and then the disfigured face of Thin Khun.

'Where are the others?'

'They arrested twelve of us. As far as I know, Kyak Kyaw and Shu managed to escape.'

Intense pain cripples my back. I am exhausted and don't even want to think. I mumble a few words before falling into a lethargic sleep.

Once again, aggressive voices echo in my head, accompanied by the sound of a nightstick hitting the bars one by one. They approach menacingly. The metal door of the cell squeaks.

'On your feet, lazy bones!'

I struggle to raise my heavy body, I am too weak. I cast a frantic look at Thin Khun and Law Win who are being hauled to their feet by two other guards. They vanish down a darkened corridor. I am hit, insulted, and dragged into another windowless room, where the only furniture is a small stool. A man is waiting for me, in fact there are two, perhaps even three.

They set about beating me until I collapse. I crawl along the floor to escape the kicking. One of them pulls me up violently by the arm and forces me to my knees. Another grabs my hair, forcing me to look upwards, nearly breaking my neck in the process. He places his hand round my throat, suffocating me before throwing me back on to the ground. They kick me again, then drag me back up onto my knees.

'The interrogation can begin.'

'Your name. Where are you from?'

'Shan State, Sir.'

'Bullshit! You're not from Myanmar, you filthy Bengali!'

The officer punches me in the face.

'Where are you from, you goddam *kalar* pig?'

'Shan State.'

He yells like a maniac. 'Where is your family?'

'I'm alone. I'm an orphan. My parents are dead.'

'I'm going to tell you who you are, you're a little prick of a *kalar*. You are an invader from Arakan. You've come here illegally. Now you're going to tell me how you did it. Who helped you?'

'Have you got family in Yangon?'

A guard covers my head with a sack, more blows, raining down from all directions that I am unable to anticipate. Questions are fired at me from all quarters, they want to know everything. I spit blood, they'll get nothing from me. But what will the others say? Admit nothing. I can no longer tell which weapons, instruments, and parts of their bodies they are using to hit me. Thirst is lacerating my throat and I'm hungry. I'm terrified, the sweat is pouring off me. I can't see anything, the jute sack is ripping my skin off with every blow to my face. They rhythmically slam their fists into my ears.

'You dog! Invader!'

I feel like a panicked animal, totally at their mercy, but I must not let anything slip. I must not say anything. I must stay strong under torture. The more I speak, the more they will want to know. A single word about my family in Arakan or Yangon and they will all be dragged off to hell. I won't give them anything. The more I speak, the more the torture would be justified. The more I speak, the less chance I have of getting out. I must resist. That is all I can do now, however painful it is. I am a Muslim, a student, from Shan, no ambitions, an orphan. Deny, deny everything. I am innocent, and those who are innocent can still hope for justice through corruption.

With my bloodied head still covered with the sack, my hands tied behind my back and attached to a bar, I become their punching ball. My feet have been put on a block of ice that is burning me and the cold is so unbearable that I have lost all feeling in my calf muscles. The cold pierces my body from the inside out. The blood in my mouth mixes with my tears. Hours go by, I can't bear it anymore. All of a sudden, I just want them to finish me off, end it all. The cell might be small, but the darkness around me plunges me into a bottomless pit. The interrogation starts up again.

'You have collaborated with protest groups and been involved in clandestine activities.'

'You come from Sittwe. Admit it!'

'Do you know how *kalars* like you are punished?'

'Please, I beg you. Help me, help me. Have mercy on me.'

'You're a Muslim. Haven't you got a God to protect you?'

'Your religion is for mangy dogs. Isn't your God here to help you?'

'Who are the organisers of the movement?'

'Who wrote the pamphlets?'

A violent blow propels me forward, but the rope around my hands does not yield. My shoulders explode.

'Little prick!'

'What is it that they call you lot, *kalars*? Answer!'

They insult me again and again. Foul words. Words that taint my religion, my family, and my people. Words designed to kill. Words that stoke their hatred and violence.

'Where did you get your information?'

'Who collects your reports?'

'Are you associated with any opposition groups? The NLD?'

I think about Dad and about my qualifications, the only thing that I might have been able to offer him in return for all his sacrifices. Should I really have got involved in national causes when survival is the most important issue for the Rohingya? Did I really have to tempt fate by wanting to be a student like all the others? I am a Rohingya. Why did I even try to be like the others?

Forty-eight hours have passed and I haven't had a drop of water to drink. I have had no respite to even think about the possibility of organising my release. It has to be bought, with money. My life depends on their greed. How can I pay them without putting my loved ones in danger? Who can I contact? All my friends are here in prison. If I give them my parents' contact details, they will be arrested. No, I cannot do that. I want to die and stop the suffering.

On the third day, a plastic cup is placed between my crippled hands. Water is life, my body is in survival mode, invincible. I want to live.

On the fourth day, death still does not come even though I am constantly begging it to take me. Life clings on stubbornly because my heart still finds the strength to beat. I have never suffered like this, and every passing hour inflicts new and unsuspected pain, more agonising than ever. The guards never weary of taking turns to beat me.

'If you want to get out of here, we need cash. Otherwise we'll send you to the military camp.'

I am only too well aware that the military camp is a one-way journey for Rohingya.

The police officers allow me one last glimpse of the possibility of negotiation. The officer calls two guards: 'Take him to his cell and remove the sack from his head. Give him a bowl of rice.'

My torturers leave me alone. My stomach growls with hunger and rumbles in anticipation of the grains of rice sliding down my throat. But the effect is nothing like I expected, and is more akin to pain than pleasure.

35

Goodbye, professor

The seventh day of the end of my life.

'Out, you filthy *kalar*! You've got a visitor.'

My heart beats fast, my chains are undone. In the corridor in front of me, my comrade Thin Khun is shuffling painfully forward. I hear footsteps behind me, and slightly turn my head. It's U Thant. I'm confused. The three of us enter a room, followed by the others, the whole group. My teacher is waiting to greet us. The sight of him throws me into complete turmoil. I detect deep compassion in his eyes; he is on the verge of tears. The police officers sit us on small stools near a window. I particularly notice the window. It is tall and wide, and looks out on the outside world, which seems to be calling me. Beyond the window are woods and freedom.

An officer keeps watch on us. Our teacher enquires after our condition. Thin Khun and I are the worst affected. Ten minutes pass before our guard withdraws to the room next door. The teacher's tone changes; he lowers his voice and speaks quickly. 'Tomorrow your case will be transferred to higher authorities and the army. Your days of provisional detention are over. I have only been able to negotiate a single solution for all of you. The officers have accepted a large sum to turn a blind eye if you escape. But it is now or never. One by one as I say your name, you must jump out of the window and run. Don't follow one another, you are on your own now. U Thant, you first.'

U Thant leaps through the open window, despite his broken arm. Before I have time to watch him vanish, the teacher signals to me.

'Nyi Nyi, go to the hostel, I'll join you there. Thin Khun, it's your turn ...'

I jump out of the window and my body is carried along by the wind of freedom, as if I had no aches and pains. I follow the path taken by U Thant, ducking under the barbed wire. It's not until I've gone another few metres that I feel the burning of the barbs on my wounds. Like all my other scars, it will take time to accept and forget. Right now, the call of freedom is stronger.

I carry on running through the woods behind the police station. I leap over banks, and race down a small hill, across two rice fields, over a wall, and find myself walking along the alleyways of Irrawaddy. I am frightened and would like to walk faster, but I am breathless and coughing. I feel stabbing pain in my wounds. I need to calm myself down.

After about an hour, I finally catch sight of the hostel. The teacher is waiting for me in my cupboard in the backyard. There is no time to lose.

'Nyi Nyi, here are a few coins to buy a bus ticket and pay for a few journeys. You must flee straightaway. Don't stay in Myanmar, they have your name on file. Take these clothes and change. Go to the bus station and travel via Yangon. You will be anonymous there, which will give you a few days to find the money you need to leave the country. Travel via the remotest areas of Shan State because the borders between Myanmar and Thailand are temporarily closed and Special Forces have been deployed to target Burmese students. Goodbye.'

I take the money, and lift his hands to my face. There is so much I want to say to him that I can't find the words.

'Professor ...'

'Go, Nyi Nyi! Leave the country as quickly as you can and don't come back as long as the junta remains in power. Don't contact any of us. They are going to issue a wanted notice. If you are identified, you will be killed. You haven't got a minute to lose.'

I put on the clothes that he has given me. I contemplate for one last time this good and level-headed man who has taught me that Burmese unity is about feeling part of a country that is made richer by recognising its differences rather than by imposing a single model.

'Goodbye, professor!'

36

Black moon over the Mekong

I am in a teahouse at the bus station, pretending to read a discarded magazine and struggling to calm my anxiety as I listen out for the call that the bus for Winnyo is about to depart. Have the authorities already issued a search warrant for me? Has the army been informed? The bus station is an escape route, but could easily be a funnel that leads directly back to their cells.

'Passengers for Winnyo! All aboard!'

The bus frenetically honks its horn, making me jump. Thick black smoke encircles the vehicle that is now in a hurry to leave. I take a seat a few rows back from the driver, press my face to the window, and keep my eyes fixed on the road. Every second that ticks by is a blessing, every mile brings temporary relief. I need to get out of this town and to Yangon as quickly as possible.

The journey progresses without mishap. Luck is smiling on me.

In Winnyo, I board a train for the capital. A few hours later, the countryside through the window gives way to the suburbs of Yangon as the train enters a small station for a brief stop. That is when I see the police officers board three carriages ahead of me, probably for an identity check. When the train gets going again, I jump out less than a kilometre before the main station. Successful escape; I am in Yangon.

I immediately take a taxi to the district where my auntie lives. The door cracks open and I see a combination of surprise and panic on her face. I enter and quickly shut the door behind me.

'I'm not staying. I have to leave the country. I need your help.'

'God protect you, my son.'

My uncle rifles through drawers and proffers a bundle of banknotes.

'Go and change half of it into foreign currency straightaway because once you're outside Myanmar, no one will accept your kyats. They will be worthless.'

After changing the money, I go to a small Muslim travel agent that my uncle has recommended. I don't need to explain that I am fleeing the country as he can easily guess my intentions from the simple fact that I am a Rohingya. He advises me to take the train up to Shan State via Mandalay, because identity checks on that line are few and far between.

Mandalay is nearly 400 miles from Yangon so this will be an interminable journey. Despite my state of exhaustion, I keep an eye out at every station. As we approach Bago, a military stop, I am extra vigilant. A dozen soldiers are waiting on the platform, loaded with bags and headed for new camps and new battles. They are about to board my carriage. I move two carriages down to one that is packed with women and families. They won't bother me here. It is a gamble, but I have no other option. Most of the passengers on this line are from the majority Bamar Buddhist ethnic group and the soldiers tend to be less suspicious.

At Mandalay station, I ask a Muslim betel vendor for information.

'Are you heading to Shan State? I'm trying to reach the Thai border.'

The man raises an eyebrow as he sips his coffee.

I add, 'I need to get through the checkpoints without the authorities checking my documents.'

After a quick discussion, we come to an agreement. I will pay him twice the going rate. I'll just have to trust him and hope for a bit of luck.

'You'll be my assistant driver,' he says. 'When we go through the checkpoints, you'll help the passengers disembark for the checks. I am a retired army officer, and I know all the soldiers. If things get tricky and they start asking you questions, say that you are my wife's brother's cousin and that you are helping me out for the day. Learn my name on my identity card, my father's name, and my address by heart. You can say that you live with me. Okay?'

'Okay.'

'Now go to the police station and get a letter of recommendation. Just tell them that you've lost your papers and give them the names that I've given you.'

Without papers, I would never get anywhere. So it is better to tackle the problem head on rather than keep a low profile. The letter will be my talisman. In the time that it takes me to go to the police station, the betel vendor has crammed as many passengers and their belongings as he can into his vehicle, and we set off for Keng Tung.

A dozen or so miles further on, the first checkpoint appears on the horizon. I feel a lump in my throat, I need to keep my composure. I jump out of the vehicle and stand in front of the door to count the passengers, speaking quite loudly to attract everyone's attention.

'Identity check! All passengers down from the bus.'

I then walk round to the bonnet and pretend to check the radiator, topping it up with water. Out of the corner of my eye, I watch the passengers being checked. The driver honks his horn, other vehicles are waiting behind us. I climb into the front of the bus, which rolls forward a few feet to pick up the passengers. I act the part of assistant again.

'All aboard!'

Once all the passengers have taken their seats, I jump into the place next to the driver. He doesn't look at me, but I detect the hint of a smile on his lips. We set off. It is a minor victory until we reach the next checkpoint on the winding mountain roads.

The bus goes through other checkpoints where the somewhat listless soldiers are mostly busy with the passengers. I feel a knot in my stomach every time we stop.

At the end of the day, we arrive in Keng Tung. The driver pockets the money that I agreed to pay and wishes me well for the onward journey. Once again, I have to go to the police station to get another travel permit that will take me closer to the border. I repeat the scenario of claiming that I have lost my papers, which works thanks to the usual small bribe, and I manage to find a place in a large freight truck transporting bricks. The journey through the mountains in Shan State takes several hours. The vehicle rattles over the rocky track, making me nauseous. Two farmers from the Shan-wa minority are travelling with me. We soon strike up a jovial conversation. Rawwa and Shu are well into their forties and have the energy of the righteous. They are both dirt poor and survive mostly from hunting and growing crops. They are not prejudiced in the slightest against my colour or origins and are extremely kind to me while remaining discreet. My presence in this truck in a remote corner of Shan State intrigues them. As we chat, I end up admitting that I am a student who is fleeing the country. Rather than condemning or shunning me as I expected, they are reassuring and sympathetic. When we reach the end of our journey and climb down from the bus, they gesture to me to follow them.

'This region is in the hands of the Shan-wa rebel army,' one of the men tells me. 'There is no need to fear the Burmese soldiers here. We help those who are trying to escape, because we live under the same repression.'

I follow them along a winding path through the jungle to their village. Shu takes me to a young man who is armed. He talks to him for a few minutes in a dialect that I don't understand before turning back to me.

'It's settled, you can follow him. Naing Oo is going to help you and take you to another village near the Mekong. You have nothing to fear from him.'

I thank God for putting such charitable people in my path.

The young man smiles at me; he does not speak Burmese. With a hand gesture, he indicates that I should get into his jeep, and we set off immediately on a long, two-hour journey. When we arrive at our destination, my driver stops in front of a hut and introduces me to U Win Htut, a man of around 60, a trader from the Wa ethnic community who frequently travels between the border areas in the Golden Triangle.[†]

---

† Laos, Thailand, and Myanmar.

U Win Htut is immediately welcoming and shows me great generosity. He offers me dishes of rice and vegetable curry to help me recover from the long distances that I've travelled in the past few days. He applies some traditional ointment to my wounds and bruises. I quickly find myself dropping off to sleep.

Later when I wake up, he is standing in front of me with an amiable expression on his face and offers to take me on a tour of the village. I feel a tugging on my heartstrings when I realise that the people here are not much richer than in Arakan and Chin State. Malaria is rife, particularly among children, and schooling appears non-existent. In spite of all this, they have big hearts.

'A student fleeing the regime is part of the resistance, you are our brother,' U Win Htut tells me.

He informs me that in the early hours of the morning hundreds of livestock will be herded onto an illegal boat on the Mekong and advises that I attempt to sneak on board with them.

The following morning, I say my farewells to U Win Htut and express my sincere gratitude. The boat is moored to the riverbank and the boatmen are preparing for departure. I slip in between the buffaloes, goats, and pigs. Destination: Thailand.

The boat glides away on the Mekong. I am in the centre of the Golden Triangle, at a crossroads in my life. Behind me: Arakan, my family, my father's hopes of making an educated man of me, the kind of man who can serve my community. I have failed and my ties are severed.

The boat finally comes ashore between Laos and Thailand. I recognise the bridge from the directions given by U Win Htut. This is where I need to disembark. Without thinking twice, I jump off the boat and head for the jungle. I walk for 30 minutes and cross the Laos border into the village of Chiang Sen in Thailand. I change the two hundred Chinese yuan that I have left from the money that I exchanged in Yangon and go in search of work. I approach a group of market traders.

'Have you got papers?'

'I've just fled Myanmar.'

Barely have I uttered these words before their faces take on closed expressions and their attitudes waver between aggression and fear.

'You should leave.'

'We don't want any Burmese here.'

'If you stay, the police will arrest you by nightfall.'

After four hours trying to find work and somewhere to stay in Chiang Sen, I realise that it is dangerous for me here and I run the risk of being escorted back to the border, which is the worst thing that could happen to me.

At the bus station, I find out that the bus for the nearest town, Chiang Rai, leaves in three days' time. It is too long to wait and it is already dark. I decide to go by foot. I walk a few hundred feet, feeling utterly lost and disoriented, with the sensation that I have been uprooted and that I am not myself anymore. I look up to the sky as if I hear it calling to me. The moon — the only connection that I still have with my home and family. This evening it is dark, a new moon, a black moon. I remember my grandma's words: *a black moon is always a bad omen.*

This evening, as new horizons beckon, the moon has chosen not to accompany me, as if it disapproves of the path that I am taking. While it stubbornly remains hidden behind thick clouds, at least their brightly lit contours are there to help me put one foot in front of the other. I am looking for signs of reassurance. On this road into the unknown, I have a difficult future ahead of me.

I have been walking for several hours when I see some headlights in the darkness. I wave my hand, the vehicle stops, picks me up, and drops me off a bit further on at the bus station in Chiang Rai.

Exhausted, I slump down on one end of a bench where three tourists are already sitting. They are all carrying heavy backpacks and are full of enthusiasm. They strike up a conversation with me, elated about their trip and eager to find out about this strange world so different from theirs. Two Australian men and an English woman who have all taken a year off to travel the world. After Thailand, they'll be exploring Indonesia, Europe, and South America. They are convinced that I am Indian. When I reveal my identity, they all look surprised. I don't match the image that they have of Burmese people. They ask me why I am here, so I tell them in so many words that I have fled the country. There is so much that I would like to say, but I keep it vague. We may be here in the same place, but our journeys are very different — theirs is all about enjoying themselves and discovering new things, and mine is about hardship and exile. They are travelling to Bangkok. With no identity card I am unable to buy a ticket. I risk asking them if they can help me. They suddenly look distrustful, but I reassure them by holding out my baht[†] and they agree to purchase my ticket for me so as not to raise the suspicions of the ticket clerk.

I am sleeping like a baby on the back seat of the bus when I feel someone shaking my arm.

'Wake up, you're in Bangkok.'

---

† Thai currency.

37

Angels in the city

Bangkok, January 2000

I leave the noise and chaos of Mo Chit bus terminal behind me as fast as I can. It is a place where buses, tuk-tuks, and mini-vans come and go at a frenzied pace, street dealers ply their trade, and all kinds of officials, outlaws, and thieves circulate. My brain is in a massive fog. Where should I go, what should I do? I am lost and virtually penniless in a country that I don't know, where they speak a language that is totally unknown to me. I walk for a long time around this gigantic, oppressive, and sprawling city. Miles of grey buildings, alleyways, streets, and boulevards. It is endless, and there is no grass, fields, or meadows. A handful of trees occasionally line a rutted pavement. Tired, injured, and forlorn dogs hang around waiting to die with no one taking the slightest bit of notice of them. I roam the streets trying to find someone or something familiar to me. Despite the fatigue, I don't dare sleep. This strange country is worrying, I am surrounded by constant noise. I don't know how to decipher people's intentions here, nor how to fit in, approach people, and make some kind of progress. I am out of my depth. All around me are imposing and lifeless buildings totally unlike any that I have ever seen. This is the modern world. Roads suspended high above my head, cars seeming to fly above ground level, dingy streets packed with two-way traffic, seekers of small and large profits, consumers and the consumed. The whole atmosphere makes me anxious, as I search for some human kindness, for another lost soul like me. I am looking for Burmese people, as they are the only ones who can help me understand this unfamiliar chaos, but there is nothing and no one to be found; everything is different.

Finally, I sit down under a small tree near the major thoroughfares and wait, watching the passers-by. Night falls.

At dawn, I approach the moto-taxi drivers.

'I'm looking for some Burmese people. Can you help me?'

No. They look away.

'Please, I have a hundred baht. Help me find some Burmese people.'

A young driver agrees to take me around the local area. I go into a few shops and ask if they know of anyone. The answer is always no.

An old man scoffs, 'The Burmese here hide under false identities, no one knows that they are Burmese. They try to pass unnoticed because of the police raids. You'll have trouble finding anyone.'

I carry on searching, asking just the one question: do you know any Burmese people? My question is often met with an aggressive look.

'Go away, you filthy parasite, or I'll call the police.'

'Get off my property!'

I make myself scarce and go further afield, as far as I can from these hostile streets, and try again. On the second evening, a woman pushing a food stall who has noticed me wandering around the neighbourhood for the past two days offers me a bowl of noodles.

'I'll help you. Follow me. I'll take you to a building site where there are often Burmese labourers.'

By the time we arrive, all the labourers have already left. The woman next to the one with the food stall, a Thai of Indian descent, takes pity on me and leads me to a Hindu temple where I can spend the night.

The following day, I set off once again on my search. I consult the map of Bangkok that the Australian tourists gave me and spot the American embassy. I head there, hoping to find refuge. I speak to the guard in English.

'I had to flee the Burmese military because my life was in danger, I'm looking for a safe place to stay. Can the embassy help me?'

The guard politely replies, 'I'm sorry, there is no asylum seekers' service here. You should go to Mae Sot or Mae La in the north of Thailand where they have refugee camps. That is the usual procedure.'

Disappointed, I am about to retrace my footsteps when a man leaning against a wall who has overheard the conversation approaches me. He offers me work in southern Thailand. It is a 48-hour journey, and I don't have the energy to start travelling again, nor do I want to put myself in the hands of this stranger. I want to find something here and now. I haven't the strength to follow a man I don't know to the other side of the country. I know nothing about him and don't trust him. I am feeling very fragile and am looking for something or someone familiar to lean on. It is a question of survival — above all else, I need to find someone who is Burmese. Exhaustion is written all over my face and this man seems overly interested in me. I prefer to decline his offer.

'I'll leave you my number. Ring me if you want.'

He hands me a piece of paper that I shove in my pocket. If I can't find anything here, I will need to have some way of feeding myself. I still want to believe that something will turn up. I can't possibly die of hunger in such a city of plenty.

I stop to sit down and rest on a low wall near a bus stop. I am totally incapable of concentrating and am falling apart mentally. My haggard appearance causes a few busy passers-by to turn and stare. The hours go by, then I notice a man wearing a Muslim chain. He is reading a newspaper while he waits for a bus, and he ends up putting it down next to him. I spot the classified ads, perhaps there is work to be found. I take the risk.

'Can I borrow your newspaper?'

'Yes of course. Where are you from?'

'Myanmar, sir.'

'What do you do here?'

'I've just arrived, sir.'

'Do you have somewhere to live?'

'No, I'm looking for work and accommodation.'

'Have you got any friends here?'

'No, I'd like to find some Burmese people.'

'Come with me, I'll introduce you to one of my employees. He is Burmese.'

We enter a clinic not far from the bus stop. The man works there, he is a doctor.

'Aung Kyaw, could you give some advice to this young man from Myanmar? He has just arrived in Thailand.'

Aung Kyaw throws me a rather disdainful look. He is a Bamar and immediately spots that I am a Rohingya. He gives me 50 baht, the price of a bowl of noodles, and the address of a *kalar* market trader, as he puts it. I pretend not to notice and thank him.

The Rohingya sells bread from a barrow in front of a shop. I walk up to him.

When he sees me, his face lights up.

'Hello, my brother. What brings you here?'

'I've just arrived and I need some advice. I'm a bit lost. I was told that you are a Rohingya. Can you recommend a place where I could sleep and find some work?'

The man scrutinises me, sounding me out, and we exchange a few pleasantries. I find it easy to understand Ramzan — his expressions, language, and way of thinking are all familiar to me. He is prepared to let me stay with him; he doesn't often meet Rohingya and if he can help me, he will. This man is my saviour.

In a tiny room in a rundown building along a sordid alleyway hidden away from the main thoroughfares, there is an old straw mattress on the ground.

'This is my bed. Please rest. There are some basins of water in the back to freshen yourself up. I'm sure you need a good wash after your long journey.'

The generosity of this humble and destitute stranger, who, without hesitation, is prepared to share what little he has with me, moves me deeply. His humanity is a rare light in the bottomless pit of despair in which I've found myself since the evening of the raid. It is a respite from this infernal spiral.

Twenty-four hours later, I wake up starving. Ramzan smiles at me kindly and brings me some rice. He then spends the next few hours explaining to me how Thailand works, what the dangers are, the identity checks, the police, the immigration services, and how to disappear in the crowd. In short, how to be accepted by the Thais.

'Ramzan, I went to the American embassy and they told me about some camps for Burmese refugees in the north of the country.'

He knows exactly what I am talking about.

'The roads are swarming with police and checkpoints. If you try and go there, the risk of being imprisoned and deported to Myanmar is much greater than the likelihood of being listed as a refugee. There is huge demand for it. I don't want to discourage you, but Rohingya rarely make it onto the list of Burmese refugees who manage to get resettled in the United States or Australia, and it's very unlikely that they'll even let you into the camp.'

Ramzan falls silent. His mind is elsewhere, back where we come from in Arakan. He tells me his story and how he came to flee Myanmar. His village was destroyed and replaced by army housing. Every member of his family was arrested and put to work. Some died and others were forced to live in the concentration-camp towns of Maungdaw and Buthidaung. He has lost contact with his parents, brothers, and sisters. He has no idea where they are, whether they have fled to other countries or are imprisoned in Myanmar. In Thailand, you have to understand the country's politics, customs, and traditions quickly. He works to try and make just enough money to buy his freedom if he is abducted. The situation could change from one minute to the next and he could find himself at the mercy of the agents.

'Who are the agents?' I ask him.

'Human traffickers. They are always on the lookout for any migrants from neighbouring countries. People like you who don't speak the language, who know nothing and have faith in humanity. Fugitives who have suffered a great deal and are fragile. Once you fall into their hands, you're a hostage and it's a living death.'

'Have you ever thought of going to Malaysia? Perhaps there is more hope for us there because they are Muslims.'

Ramzan sighs.

'Habib, it's been ten years since I fled the horror of Arakan. I thank God for saving me but these ten years in exile have been ten years when all I've done is survive from day to day. You can be arrested at any time, whether you're in Malaysia or Thailand, it doesn't make any difference.'

The sadness shows on his face. The ten years of fear, solitude, and pain are reflected in his eyes.

I need to contact my family to tell them that I am alive and a long way from Myanmar. Ramzan lends me a few coins to call from a phone box.

'Hello. Dad?'

'Habib, is that you?'

'I'm in Bangkok, Dad. It's a long story. I had no choice. I wanted to reassure you that I'm well.'

A long silence follows.

I know, Dad — telling you this hurts me too. I want to be with you all. What else can I tell you apart from that I am at the end of my tether, desperately sad, and utterly homesick?

'Dad?'

'God protect you, my son. Now that you've left Myanmar, it will be hard for you to return. The further away you go, the more the road back will be strewn with pitfalls. The only peace that a Rohingya can have is inner peace. Take care to protect that.'

He continues by imploring me to always stay in contact with them because I am the eldest, the only one who can take his place if something happens to him. He explains to me that I am the pillar of our family and that, now that I am abroad, I have to carry on helping them because they are barely surviving. He ends with some advice about always sticking to my principles and this sentence that will forever be engraved on my mind: 'You are a Rohingya, son. Never forget that.'

I am distraught. I go back and lie on Ramzan's mattress on the ground without saying a word. Dad always knows more than I tell him. He has this gift, or perhaps he knows the story of the Rohingya past, present and future only too well. Can the cyclical nature of history be broken? Can I hope for a destiny other than the one that was laid down for me?

I shut my eyes and imagine that I am there with them. No, I won't forget them, they will always be there in the deepest part of my heart and I must stay near them, near you, Dad. I will not be a burden to you or cause you sorrow. I will be the solution, sooner or later. I promise, Dad.

38

Escape

It is 24 January 2000. Ramzan comes running up to me.

'Put the bread in the sack and leave your barrow. Quick!'

In a flash, we grab our produce and head for the railway line. Ramzan dives into the thickets alongside the tracks and drags me into his extraordinarily well-concealed but fetid hideout in a place where no one would ever expect human beings to hide. All around us, the police are combing apartments and shops. We stay in our cesspit for several hours, without budging. Once things quieten down, Ramzan tells me to return to the room. He comes back a while later. I have prepared him a bowl of rice with some herbs found in some abandoned cardboard boxes at the market. He holds out a magazine written in English.

'Habib, read this. I don't understand everything, but it concerns us. The two kids from God's Army have got themselves in the papers. They are on all the front pages.'

I start reading the article in the daily newspaper. Two Burmese children have in fact hit the headlines. Their names are Johnny and Luther Htoo, who at just eleven years old have been the leaders of the Karen army of Christian guerrillas known as God's Army since 1997. They have become notorious for their fight against the Burmese junta at the Thai border. They are said to have magic powers including immunity to bullets and landmines. Legend has it that the two children have 400,000 invisible soldiers under their command as well as 300 men who live monastic lives with no sex, alcohol, milk, eggs, or pork. The twins ordered the taking of hostages in a hospital in Ratchaburi in western Thailand to draw attention to the Karens' plight. Eight hundred people including patients and hospital staff were held hostage for 22 hours by ten members of the organisation. In return for the hostages' release, God's Army demanded freedom for their people. The Thai Army organised a commando operation and the ten men were killed. The Thais have set the dogs on us.

'What do you think, Ramzan?'

'The authorities have been very active in the past few days and the raids are likely to intensify. The situation looks like it will degenerate, and there is increasing mistrust and hatred of Burmese migrants. It doesn't look good for us.'

During the night, a number of arrests are made a few streets away from us. We run from place to place hiding in the huge holes in the Bangkok streets where foul-smelling waste water is discharged.

But with the increasing frequency of the raids, it is becoming impossible to move, much less earn a living.

'If you are arrested, Habib, you will be handed over to the Burmese Army.'

A sudden image of prison and torture appears in my head.

'I have ten years' experience living in Thailand. My intuition is rarely wrong. We are not safe in the current climate, more and more people are being denounced to the police. The neighbours know that I am Burmese, they could report us.

'Isn't there a Muslim country that might be more lenient towards us?'

'Oh, my dear brother, Malaysia is a Muslim country but there is no way in the world that I would want to go back there. I can't tell you which country might be the most welcoming for stateless people like us. I've been in many places and each one is as horrendous as the next.'

We will have to part ways. I have to save my skin, staying would be pure madness. I can see only one possible solution as things stand — contacting the man who offered to send me to Golok in southern Thailand. I am about a hundred baht short if I want to leave immediately. Ramzan willingly gives me the money. I will never be able to thank him enough for his generosity.

'Goodbye, my brother.'

I leave Ramzan and Bangkok, heading south.

39

The rickety bridge

Golok bus terminal, 25 January 2000

I leave the bus station and head for the centre of town. The atmosphere seems strange and I suddenly feel panicky. I remember Ramzan's advice: 'The authorities have eyes everywhere, they know everything. Behave like the locals if you want to avoid being noticed. When you're working, watch the other workers and do what they do. Camouflage is your only protection. Stop wearing a *longyi* and wear trousers.'

My brain is completely scrambled, and I have lost the phone number of the man I met in front of the American embassy. One false move and I will be exposed, arrested by the Thai authorities, and deported to Myanmar, straight into the arms of my persecutors. Torture then death. I chase these thoughts away — the anxiety on my face will betray me. I need to look ahead, think clearly, and find a solution.

Two police officers appear behind me. I gather my wits,

hurry towards the entrance of a five-storey building, and disappear into the stairwell. It's a hotel. The police officers summon some colleagues who respond almost immediately. I can hear them running after me.

There are toilets at the end of the corridor. As I slip behind one of the doors, I catch the eye of a cleaning woman emerging from another cubicle at exactly the same moment. She walks towards the men as they pound along the corridor. My heart is beating fast. I whisper a prayer that the woman will be kind to me. She points at the stairs up to the next floor. I am dripping with sweat. I bless her.

I stay in the toilets for half an hour. The woman comes back and signals to me that the coast is clear. I give her a look full of gratitude. She holds out her hand palm upwards and shakes it vigorously, indicating that she wants money. I dig around in my pockets and give her everything I have left, 50 baht.

I wander the streets, thinking. I have to act fast; I have nothing to eat and nowhere to sleep.

I pass a small shop on the ground floor of a faded apartment block. An old man beckons to me through the window. I glance back and catch sight of uniforms coming around the corner and the decision is made for me. I swiftly enter the shop and hide behind the shelves. The old man smiles at me and I smile back. He has understood. He offers me some tea and I take advantage of his hospitality to use his telephone. Ramzan has given me the number of another potential employer in Golok called Chalem.

The man on the other end of the line agrees to give me work immediately. I breathe a sigh of relief. An hour later, Chalem honks his horn outside the shop and gestures to me to get into his car. Soon, we arrive at the Thai customs post.

'This is your new place of work. Everything is arranged. You can come and go safely. You need to set up in the middle of the bridge on the Thai side.'

Chalem makes and sells gift boxes filled with jasmine flowers and biscuits. He explains to me that the bridge is a good place to do business because people cross every day from Malaysia to Thailand, and fresh jasmine is a popular lucky charm. It is also a nice souvenir to buy for family and friends on the way back from a trip across the border. The homemade biscuits that accompany the bouquets are baked by Chalem's nieces. He gives me a bundle of 30 or so of these little jasmine decorations.

As I handle the flowers, I inhale their fragrance. It reminds me of Mum and her delicate hands. I miss her so much! Thinking about the distance between us drives me crazy. I wipe away the tears that have started rolling down my cheeks and set to work.

To my right are the Malaysian authorities, and to my left the Thai authorities. I wish myself invisible. So far so good. Soldiers and customs officers patrol under the bridge, and appear astonishingly indifferent to me and the dozen other vendors by the roadside. I convince myself that once again my attitude will make all the difference. In a gesture intended to show confidence, I hold out my flowers and biscuits to try to tempt travellers weary of waiting their turn to have their documents checked.

On this rickety bridge between the two countries on either side of the Golok River, I am precariously balanced as if on a tightrope. Men and women come and go from one side to the other, skipping freely from one country to another, totally unaware of the enormous privilege that their passports bestow. I wobble in the middle of this fragile footbridge, stateless, dreaming that one day I too will be able to cross borders with documents like everyone else, and that I too will be free, but knowing that I could fall into the lions' den at any moment.

In the evening, Chalem comes to fetch me, collect the takings, and prepare the barrow for the next day. He offers me a place to sleep in a small hut next to his chicken coop, a short distance from Golok.

By the fourth day, I feel more at ease. Sales generate more sales, and travellers are now more likely to approach me of their own accord.

As I am greeting my last customers of the day, a Malaysian guard beckons me over. I hesitate, before walking towards him.

'Passport!'

Other officers are accosting the vendors who work alongside me. The cabins used for identity checks are full to bursting. I end up being taken with four bread-sellers to an area next to a railway track where a jeep is parked. The guards stand there cracking their knuckles. Two of them take me to one side and address me in their language, which I struggle to understand, although what they are saying is obvious from their aggressive tone and gestures. One of them orders to me to sit on the ground, then kicks me in the forehead, while a second thumps me in the back. Next to me, two other officials are pummelling the chest and shoulders of another vendor. For Muslims, the forehead, chest, and shoulders are sacred parts of the body, because it is through them that one communicates with God. These men know exactly where to hurt us.

We are taken to a military camp before being transferred to the police post in Kelantan, in the far north of Malaysia, where we spend the night. The following morning, we are handed over to the commandos at Tanah Merah camp. The admission procedures begin. The guards walk around us and order us to remove our clothing. We are completely naked.

'Bend over!'

Several of us react indignantly.

'You can't ask us to do that. It's degrading.'

'It is against the rules of our religion. You are Muslims too. You must know that it is not allowed.'

The punches fly and we are subjected to humiliating full-body searches.

Each of us is given a number and we are taken to a large hall packed with hundreds of other prisoners from all over Malaysia. It is a nightmarish sight. I am caught in the middle of this nauseating mass of sweaty flesh, people stuck together like cattle in a herd.

A week goes by and the camp empties and fills again like a human accordion. I just try to keep my head together and maintain my inner balance in this chaos. I close my eyes, breathe, and try to shut out the present, maintain my dignity, and wait for whatever happens next.

It is 5 February 2000. The immigration officers have decided to get rid of me and around 80 other Burmese prisoners. Our turn comes at nightfall. In groups of 12 per minibus, we are taken to a customs post on the Malaysian border. Papers are brandished; we sign our names on the list. We are officially deported to Thailand. The officers force us to walk towards a bridge that will take us back over the border. One of the prisoners starts panicking, followed by a second, and then it spreads to the rest of the group. Several throw themselves at the officers' feet and beg on their knees, hands clasped together.

'Please don't hand us over to the Thai border officials! They'll send us back to Myanmar and the army will kill us.'

Some of them extract a few concealed banknotes from the seams of their trousers and soles of their shoes.

'Please, take all our money, but don't make us go over there.'

Belts, shoes, money ... Everyone makes a small contribution. I have nothing. Fortunately, the booty appears to make them relent.

One of the officers makes a telephone call. We walk around the bridge to a small passageway below. Men dressed in civilian clothing are waiting for us and instruct us to board some small boats.

'Crouch down in the bottom of the boat, and stay hidden from view. Not a sound!'

Once we have been camouflaged, the boatmen make their way upriver and deposit us on the riverbank next to Golok Mosque. There, armed men order us to climb onto the backs of their motorbikes two by two.

'Get a move on! The police are nearby. Come on!'

None of us think to argue. I climb onto the back of a motorbike. I am afraid that they are human traffickers; their intentions are not yet clear.

Once we arrive in a safe place a bit further on, all is revealed.

'We've helped you to avoid the police, now you need to pay us. Two options: either you have friends, or you don't. If you don't, we'll find you work on the fishing boats or in the markets. Our conditions will apply.'

The traffickers threaten us and rough a few of us up to encourage us to think quickly. I receive a stinging slap. We are allowed the use of a telephone to try to raise some money. I contact Chalem who replies sharply that he can do nothing. He already had to pay the Thai border guards to turn a blind eye to my presence on the bridge. I must have got too close to the

Malaysian side. I have one last resort — my father in Myanmar. I remember that he once mentioned some friends in Malaysia.

I keep it brief on the phone — I don't want to worry him.

'Dad, I'm at the Thai border. I need around six hundred ringgit[†] to cross the border into Malaysia or I will be sent to prison. Have you got a friend in Malaysia who can help me?'

'Habib, my son, there is my friend Hassan from Sittwe. I'll call him and tell him what's happened. Be careful, Habib. Call me when you're out of trouble.'

'Don't worry, Dad. Everything will be all right, it will all be sorted soon. I will take care of everything. I have to go.'

Hassan later tells me that he is broke, but that he might have a solution — one of his employers might be prepared to pay me an advance if I agree to work for him when I get to Malaysia. I eagerly accept.

Three days later, Hassan informs the traffickers that the money is ready and that they will be given it once I arrive safely in Kuala Lumpur. Six hundred ringgit is the price to escape slavery on the Thai seas. The price of a reprieve.

We leave at midnight the same day, travelling by car, boat, and then on foot through the jungle. Ten shadowy figures in the night among the ferns and palm leaves. Running, walking, stopping suddenly, standing motionless, and holding our breath before setting off again. Trying to ignore the fact that the jungle is full of wild animals like snakes and tigers, as well as the man-hunters who are tracking and lying in wait for us. Dawn finally breaks. We reach Bukit Kwong Dam where a car is waiting for us. We squeeze into the boot and, after two hours of near asphyxia, we arrive in Kota Bharu. There are still hundreds of miles to go.

---

† Malay currency.

40

Kuala Lumpur, ten men in the night

Our escape through the border jungles and along the Malaysian highways finally ends in a gloomy car park in a Kuala Lumpur suburb. Hassan is there waiting with another man. My benefactor hands the ransom over to the traffickers. Once the money is counted out, the car door is opened, two of us step out at our final destination, and the vehicle, along with the other Burmese passengers, vanishes into the distance. I have already erased them and the whole horrendous episode from my memory. A new life in a new country begins.

Hassan is the same age as my dad. As we walk through the city, he tells me stories about Arakan, my father, and their teenage years. His eyes light up as he recalls their fishing trips. He describes life in Arakan as it once was: his childhood during a period of calm between two ethnic cleansing operations — before the curse of the Rohingya struck again — and then the witch hunt that forced him to flee. He suddenly becomes serious and fires questions at me. I tell him about Sittwe, my escape, and the circumstances that brought me here. The eternal suffering of the Rohingya in Myanmar, where nothing ever changes for those who remain.

Golden light reflects off the magnificent mosque in Kuala Lumpur city centre. The soft sound of chanting from the minarets echoes reassuringly between the modern buildings. A source of comfort. At least here I won't be blamed for being born a Muslim. Hope springs in my heart. A whole range of possibilities suddenly unfolds before me again. All the dreams that I once had — making something of my life, studying, and being able to send money to my parents.

Hassan takes me to the building site where the employer who paid my ransom is waiting for me. I am committed to working there for several months with no wages to pay him back. I join the team of a hundred men cutting marble paving stones for a luxury hotel in Negeri Sembilan. Half are Indonesians, the others are Burmese from the Chin and Rohingya ethnic groups. I find somewhere to sleep with a few other labourers, in an abandoned container that offers sparse comfort. The work is hard and the sun beats down on us. After a few days, the nightmare begins again.

'*Operasi! Operasi!*†'

A couple of hundred feet away, men in white T-shirts clasping metal bars jump out of a truck and run towards us.

The foreigners and refugees on the building site disperse chaotically, shouting. Everyone drops whatever he is doing and tries to escape from the men dressed in white — commandos, soldiers, and a handful of police and immigration officers whose job it is to hunt down illegal immigrants. We dash around

† '*Operation*' in Malay.

looking for somewhere to hide, or some flat ground where we can make our escape. Three men next to me disappear into a lift and haul themselves up into the false ceiling. It takes me half a second to realise that there is no room for me to hide with them. I climb the stairs of an emergency exit four by four. I go up five, six, or maybe seven floors — I'm not sure how many exactly — I just keep climbing higher and higher. *Remember, you are a highlander, Habib.* I can hear their angry steps behind me. There are three of them, a band of hunters in pursuit of their prey. I spot an opening, leap onto the flat roof, and, without thinking, crawl into the ventilation shafts where I stay very still. They are going to catch me. My limbs go numb and my foot is trapped under my thigh. I try to mask the pain, ignore the cramp in my leg, and breathe slowly. I can hear footsteps coming and going on the roof. My heartbeat reverberates so loudly in my eardrums that I am convinced it can be heard from miles away. I lie down, dazed and exhausted. I shut my eyes and pray.

The hours go by and gradually the labourers dare to surface from their hiding places in the surrounding jungle, false ceilings, sewage outlets, pipes, excavator buckets, and under vehicles, among others. We emerge from the shadows like zombies in a deserted building site. One hundred and fifty workers — Burmese, Indonesian, Pakistani, and Bangladeshi — have been arrested and taken away in big navy-blue trucks.

The following day, the missing refugees and migrants are replaced by new labourers. Work carries on at the same pace, but I keep my wits about me. There are three million migrants in Malaysia, and as many sources of information and advance warnings. Workers with mobile phones sometimes receive text messages that the authorities are about to raid a particular building site or accommodation. Everyone then immediately downs tools and makes a beeline for the jungle. Dozens of lives are saved in this way. The nights when we decide to sleep outside rather than in our squats become increasingly frequent. Fatigue, insufficient food, stress, and the illegal working conditions often cause accidents. Many men lose their lives; death is always snapping at our heels.

41

Malaysia: my new home

Six months have passed since I arrived in Malaysia. Six months with no wages while I clear my debt. I doubt that I will be paid after this, so I decide to leave without saying anything and join Hla Myint, a Rohingya, also from Sittwe, who I met on the building site. He helps me to find a job on a BASF Petronas project. Together with some other Burmese labourers, we build a small, discreet hut out of plastic sheets behind a village called Kampung Selamat on the jungle's edge, a short distance from the beach. We avoid spending too much time there so as not to upset the locals, who are not happy about our presence; we just use it as a place to sleep. The text warnings that we receive in the middle of the night help us to avoid the worst. The sea, forests, and plantations all around us serve as escape routes and hiding places, and we often finish the night between a couple of boulders on the beach or lying on a bed of moss in the depths of the jungle being eaten alive by all kinds of insects.

On other occasions, we are woken by the immigration vans. Not everyone manages to escape.

In April 2001, a thousand soldiers surround the building site I am working on. The site managers try to use their influence to stop them entering. They have told us previously that we cannot sleep on site. They don't want to be accused of providing accommodation for illegal workers. But we don't have anywhere else to go and now we're trapped. The soldiers cart off the refugees and immigrants whose papers are not in order. I am forced to hide in an enormous water tank for several days.

In June the following year, another building site that I am working on is blockaded by the authorities for four days. Three hundred men and women are taken away, and I only just escape. I return to the abandoned container that a dozen of us are using as makeshift accommodation and protection.

Through meeting other Rohingya at various building sites, I sense a renewed spark of hope spreading amongst us. A last-ditch lifeline has arrived in the form of the United Nations Refugee Agency in Kuala Lumpur, a new branch set up in 2001 to provide assistance to refugees from Southeast Asia. They have the power to issue a UNHCR temporary protection letter, which specifies that the individual is considered a refugee and under the protection of UNHCR. In spite of the endless cycle of arrests, detentions, deportations, nights disturbed by the fear of raids, and cries for help from sons, daughters, and parents held by traffickers, the Rohingya in Malaysia will not be defeated. They set up groups — including the Myanmar Ethnic Rohingya Human Rights Organisation Malaysia — aimed at promoting a semblance of unity, and establish a dialogue between the UNHCR and those who arrive from Arakan wounded, traumatised, and lost. Rohingya living across Malaysia pass on the information by word of mouth, and it gradually circulates around building sites, detention centres, workplaces, cafes, jungles, and squats.

2001 heralds a small victory — the UNHCR grants Burmese refugee status to a few thousand Rohingya. Only a few dozen had previously been given this protection after a long struggle.

I am introduced to Kyaw Soe Aung, a Rohingya colleague of the brother of a friend from one of the building sites. He has been in Malaysia for eight years.

'We're going to arrange a meeting for you with the UNHCR. You will be given a temporary protection letter. It does not guarantee your safety in Malaysia, but we are hoping to finally be allowed to participate in the resettlement programmes in democratic countries, like other Burmese refugees do. Our community needs to be rebuilt, we need to have access to education and opportunities for the future,' he tells me.

This notion makes me nostalgic and overcome with melancholy. University — the dreams that Dad and I once shared.

Kyaw Soe Aung calls me back a few months later — I have an appointment at the UNHCR office. I leap with joy on hearing the news.

The night after his call, a few days before the appointment, I have a dream. I dream that I obtain a university qualification and show it to Dad. In Myanmar, a free democratic Myanmar.

The doors of the United Nations offices are closed. The guard tells me that no requests are currently being dealt with. I protest that I have an appointment. He checks his list and lets me into the building where I join a queue of men, women, and children.

When my turn comes, I am ushered into a small room where an official questions me.

'Name, age, ethnic group. It's Rohingya, isn't it? When did you arrive here? How can we get in touch with you?'

I leave the office stunned by the brevity of the interview. I would have liked to tell him about everything that has happened to me. I would have liked to tell him about Arakan, our land that was confiscated, the arrests, imprisonment, the humiliation and torture, my house that was stolen, and the continuing persecution of my family who are held hostage under the apartheid system in Sittwe. I would have liked to be asked how I feel, what my needs are. If I had somewhere to sleep, if I was hungry, about my state of health. I would have liked all kinds of things because I feel alone, hunted, and sad; I would have liked a listening ear, some empathy. I would have liked some comfort because I don't know where to turn anymore. I am tired of being on edge, day after day, a ball of stress in my stomach, with no respite, in a world where a single lapse of concentration could turn my life upside down. Because I am my mother's and my father's son and I miss my family. Because I am a man like any other.

Despite all this, something changes inside me.

I have a status. I have been declared a refugee.

The persecutions I have suffered are now recognised.

I stare at the letter for hours.

I am under the protection of the United Nations.

I will exist.

Finally.

42

From one hell to another

Unfortunately, this is far from the end of it. The letter from the United Nations grants me a status, but does not afford any real protection.

In 2004, after being arrested and held several times in immigration detention centres in Malaysia, then sold by Malay and Thai immigration officers to human traffickers, who sold me on to a mafia of Thai fishermen, I become a slave in the Andaman Sea. We work mostly at night. Crabs and shrimp flail around in our nets. We are not given a moment's respite. They threaten to throw us overboard if the work is not done. Huge numbers of Burmese refugees disappear at sea. I take my life in my hands and manage to escape during a short stop at Ranong Port in western Thailand, abandoning the other slaves to their tragic fates.

I return to Kuala Lumpur, where I started. A band of volunteer citizens called the RELA[†], consisting of 500,000

---

† *Ikatan Relawan Rakyat Malaysia*, The People's Volunteer Corps in Malaysia.

militia, are engaged in a gigantic manhunt. After drugs, migrants are public enemy number two in Malaysia. Even today, for each illegal worker caught — including refugees with United Nations status — RELA members receive a substantial bonus. I dream of returning home, to where I grew up and where my loved ones are. Mum and Dad are being increasingly harassed by the Rakhines and the authorities. I try to stay in touch with them as much as I can. Babuli has been forced to leave Arakan. He was caught crossing the border into Bangladesh and thrown into jail to rot. It took Mum and Dad a year and a half to raise enough money to negotiate his release. He was then forced to flee alone. A solitary fugitive, whose own personal labyrinth took him in the opposite direction to mine, to Nepal.

Four years later, my father is imprisoned for the twelfth time. He spends six months behind bars, during which time he is relentlessly tortured and assaulted by prison officers. He is utterly spent. Sounding exhausted, he just about manages to tell me on the phone that one of my sisters made it to Yangon, where she is in hiding, keeping her origins secret. Babuli has apparently since been forced to leave Nepal and possibly entered China illegally, but Dad doesn't really know and has received no more news of him.

A while later, in February, Mum calls me in tears. Dad is dead. He never recovered from the torture that was inflicted on him in prison. My heart instantly shatters into tiny pieces; my face tenses up, I sweat, I go from boiling hot to freezing cold, and finally I collapse onto the floor. Images of him and of my childhood flash through my mind. The love of my life, my reason for living. My father, my role model, my hero.

43

Whistleblowers

Despite the constant threats, I renew contact with former comrades to organise community and activist networks in Kuala Lumpur. From 2006 onwards, I begin to understand the mechanics of life as an illegal migrant, and this gives me a certain degree of self-confidence that enables me to slip through the net more easily. Through relationships with NGOs and journalists, I demand my rights, those of my community in Malaysia, and, more particularly, in Myanmar, where my loved ones are still subject to what I am not alone in calling a slow genocide. Thanks to friends who lend me money to pay the ransoms, I escape death and arrests, and find the energy to demonstrate in front of embassies, write press releases on behalf of the Rohingya Association to which I belong, and give a few interviews to independent journalists who are interested in our cause. Improvisation, mutual aid, and faith are all we have to survive. I accept without hesitation any opportunity to speak to the media and highlight the persecution of the Rohingya in Myanmar and throughout Southeast Asia, particularly in Malaysia and Thailand, where many of us are losing our lives in jungles in the border areas. If my friends and I do not do this, the world will forget us, because too many walls have been built to isolate us. It is imperative that we speak out.

I take more and more risks and, on several occasions, am involved in documentaries filmed by Malaysian and French television producers. I also act as a guide for foreign photographers. I want to show them everything, but this is not without its dangers. Denouncing the trafficking of human beings is to denounce systematic corruption in which government officials are widely implicated. My comrades and I are increasingly under surveillance by the authorities who see our actions as a direct attack on the country's immigration policy. On several occasions, I am summoned by government special agents who question me on my activities. More than ever, I am under threat of arrest, not only for being an illegal immigrant but also under the Internal Security Act (ISA), which is used by the state to silence anyone considered a security threat. It allows the police to detain suspects without trial or criminal charges, by order of the Minister of the Interior.

On 20 November 2009, a documentary called *Refugees for Sale* by the British television broadcaster Channel 4 — for which I acted as fixer — is widely aired as part of their *Unreported World* series. It involves multiple revelations and shocking images. The violence of certain officials is laid bare before millions of viewers; nothing is left unsaid. My involvement and testimonial are the last straw. I am a Rohingya for whom freedom of speech does not exist, and this time I have taken my denunciations and demands too far.

I am left with no choice but to cut off my phone and flee. My only option is to try to reach Australia by sea.

44

Christmas Island

A boat is about to set sail for Indonesia from Klang in southwest Malaysia. This will be the first leg of my journey to Australia. Nine other Rohingya join the expedition.

We are hiding in bushes on the edge of the jungle. The small motorboat slowly approaches, barely troubling the still surface of the water. A man is steering it with a long bar. The squealing and creaking of the vessel betray its age. The people smuggler signals to us to come out of the thickets, climb aboard, and find a place in the open hold at the front, where space is restricted by the motor encased in a thin plywood box. We are told to camouflage ourselves so that we are hidden from view, as passengers will be boarding in a few hours and we are likely to come across a number of officials in the next few days.

There then ensues a long and appalling journey. The engine noisily spews black, foul-smelling smoke that we breathe into our lungs. We are painfully cramped and our limbs go numb.

The heat is stifling under the plastic cover. We finally arrive at our destination port. It is December 2009. We prepare to board another small motorboat, heading for Australia, with an Indonesian minor at the helm.

The journey starts auspiciously but, once we are out on the open seas, the Indian Ocean becomes increasingly menacing. After a few days, we find ourselves on raging, stormy seas. Some of the passengers are begging to return to *terra firma*, but there is no way we can turn back. The waves crash incessantly against the hull and splash onto the deck. Soaked to the bone, we cling on desperately to avoid being swept overboard and drowned in the depths of the ocean. The first engine packs up, followed by the second. The boat is spun and tossed about like a compass gone mad, but we eventually manage to get back on course, heading into terrifying walls of waves. The ocean is stronger than us. Driven by an instinct for survival, some of the group try to make a small sail with pieces of fabric. I attempt to read the maps while others try to fix the engines, without success. The men bail litres of water out of the boat in a stubborn refusal to be swallowed up so easily by the ocean. We spend the night drifting. At dawn, our young captain cries, 'Look! Birds! Australian ones.'

We are exhausted and starving. I am horribly thirsty. Most of us have already said our final prayers. I have thrown into the sea the few stones that I was carrying in my pockets, in memory of my grandmother and her stories of sailors. Suddenly, a different kind of noise can be heard above the tumultuous thundering waves and the whistling of the icy wind. A mechanical noise. The sound of an engine that rekindles our hopes. A helicopter appears on the horizon. We jump up and down waving our arms. Please let them see us! Please come and rescue us! After flying around us a few times, it disappears. An hour goes by. Anxiety begins to set in and the general euphoria is fading when a huge ship can be seen heading straight for us, the Australian Navy patrol boat ACPB *88*. The rescue operation begins. The Australians haul us aboard, wrap us in towels, give us something to eat and drink, a brief medical check, and some warm clothes. I am the only one who can speak English and I translate for the others to answer the officer's questions about where we come from and where we have travelled from.

For the first time in our lives, the authorities treat us with dignity, respect, and compassion.

Am I dreaming?

The day after 25 December, we are on our way to the detention centre on Christmas Island. I am given a new identity and will henceforth be known as Habiburahman-1979 512–03C-00571 MAL-001 Sg-(HABIB).

Deep down, I feel happy simply to be alive. I am ready to be reborn.

45

The death of a people

In May 2010, I am once again recognised as a refugee by the United Nations. It is official, and this time it is the first step in the process of being reborn as a free man.

In the meantime, my compatriots — the other exiles — and I have been transferred to the immigration detention centre in Darwin, which is much less spacious than the one on Christmas Island. As time passes and our cases become bogged down in the limbo of red tape, my hopes and dreams fade. The feeling of freedom disintegrates. The men miss their wives and children. Powerless and kept under lock and key, they worry and complain of being stuck and unable to help their families. Despair and depression set in.

The Myanmar dictatorship is still casting its long shadow over us and continuing to destroy our lives. We are human debris washed up on the Australian coast, a long way from regaining our dignity. In this cage where we are being assessed, we lose faith in justice. For us, democracy is a mirage. In this day and age, when modern lifestyles place so much emphasis on not wasting a single minute, our time does not count. We are struck by the bitter realisation that there is no peaceful place on the planet for us Rohingya.

On 20 June 2011, World Refugee Day, I clamber up the walls of my prison onto the roof. I have only one freedom left to me — the decision to stop eating. I begin a hunger strike. I want people to know about my agony and suffering. A handful of local journalists report on my protest. The only thing that stops me going mad is the idea that my family and my community, who are suffering all kinds of torture in Myanmar, only have us, the diaspora, those living in exile, to help them. We must stand up and be counted and broadcast their cries for help. From now on, I live only for them.

I have internet access in the detention centre and write to NGOs, lawyers, and journalists denouncing the treatment of all Rohingya wherever they are. But I am only one small voice. In Myanmar, as they applaud the opening up of a country that claims it is on the path to democracy, no one seems to be paying any attention to the warning signs of worse to come, except the Rohingya themselves. Large numbers of monks take to the streets in Myanmar to demonstrate against our right to exist. We try to alert public opinion to this drama, which has been going on for over 50 years, but how can the word of the Rohingya carry any credibility against the sacred word of she who is adulated throughout the world: Aung San Suu Kyi, winner of the Nobel Peace Prize? Without her support, no one will take any notice of us. Despite her continuing silence, we still believe in this woman for whom we feel deep respect, and we cling to the hope that she will take political action to save the Rohingya.

In April 2012, groups of Rakhines go from village to village in Arakan waving flags glorifying Hitler and Nazism. Some celebrate the coming of a new era by washing the statue of Buddha with blood. They no longer bother hiding their hatred and desire to get rid of us once and for all.

The massacre comes several weeks later.

It requires a pretext. On 28 May 2012, the rape and murder of a young Rakhine woman, Ma Thida Htwe, triggers a campaign of anti-Muslim propaganda. Three young Muslim men, Htet Htet, Mahmud Rawpi, and Khochi, are arrested and sentenced to death after a hasty and highly questionable investigation. Htet Htet dies in prison a few days after his arrest. A network of government workers and extremist monks inflame the internet by spreading images of the young woman alongside anti-Muslim hate speech. A village of Rakhines organises an ambush of a bus full of Muslims. The passengers are forced off the bus and beaten to death in total impunity by a furious crowd. The photographs of the disfigured corpses of these innocents are widely shared. The Rohingya population is in shock and takes to the streets to protest. The repercussions are immediate. The army and the Rakhines surround Rohingya villages and set them on fire, massacring any who try to escape with swords and blows from rifle butts. Mum and my sisters are under siege, trapped in the middle of a pogrom that is setting western Myanmar ablaze. I am constantly haunted by images of them and my aunts, uncles, cousins, and neighbours, their eyes shining with tears and blood, their stifled cries as they flee. It becomes a blur in my mind. They need me now more than ever.

Hour after hour, I wait for the news to come in. News that becomes more appalling and terrifying by the minute. Rest is impossible. I cannot sleep at night and my days are filled with darkness. We burst into tears on the phone. My friends and family everywhere are crying out for help and I can hear their voices cracking with the sheer horror of it all. They are being hunted down in the prison-state and concentration-villages in the depths of Myanmar, out of reach of help.

I am stuck. I pummel the walls of my cell in rage. These unfeeling, rough walls that prevent me from going to save them. I yell until I lose my senses. The taboo of our community that still cannot be named must be broken. Only we know what is really happening in Arakan and only we are calling this massacre by its real name: genocide. The world is unwilling to use the term, because then it would be forced to act. There is no access on the ground and the international community is reluctant to give credit to the testimonials of Rohingya survivors, which in any case are difficult to obtain, and therefore prefers to refer to it as an 'intercommunal conflict', adopting the Myanmar government's version of events, which allows them to hide the truth and justify the military operations. Our people are dying because of racial hatred. I witness this from afar, powerless to do a thing.

I find out that Rohima managed to escape to Yangon with her husband just before our village was set on fire and the bloodshed began, but one of our uncles, who was caught fleeing Arakan, revealed under torture where she and other members of the family were hiding. Rohima was arrested immediately.

My mother, Habibah, and Nojum escaped death but were displaced and herded along with hundreds of thousands of Rohingya into the concentration camps in Sittwe. They remained there for over a year and a half, at risk of disease and famine, and in fear of their lives. In 2014, my mother and Nojum tried to escape. But they were both arrested as they made their way separately to Yangon, and imprisoned for almost a year and a half in the notorious Insein prison where a truly unimaginable fate awaits Muslim women. Nojum has been scarred for life.

I have been released from the immigration detention centre in Darwin and now live in a Melbourne suburb. I am still stateless, have no passport, and am forbidden to travel. My situation is precarious, but I can work and I can fight for my family. I was able to raise enough money for friends in Myanmar to bribe the prison guards before Mum and Nojum were brought to trial. They were eventually freed a few months apart, and Mum was once again sent to the camps in Sittwe. Our friends paid a huge sum to negotiate Rohima's release in Yangon. She acquired false papers to conceal her real identity. In 2015, she managed to escape into exile in Norway, while Nojum fled to Australia, where she is currently seeking asylum.

After several appalling months in the concentration camps in Arakan, witnessing the deaths of other Rohingya on a daily basis, my mother managed to escape by bribing a few police officers, before once again being arrested and tortured. She is now just another anonymous and desperate fugitive in Myanmar, where she runs the risk of being denounced at any moment.

The massacres and indescribable violence continue. Rohingya villages are razed to the ground; soon there will be none left. Women are systematically raped, or eviscerated if they are pregnant, and their babies thrown into fires; men are arrested, murdered, and dumped in common graves. We are stripped of all humanity, and the vast majority of the population applauds this butchery because they see us as no more than vermin. The army justifies its actions by labelling the Rohingya terrorists. In October 2016, they launched Operation *Nay Myay Chin Lin Yay* (literally, Total Liquidation or Total Cleansing of the Land). But it is only since 25 August 2017, when over 600,000 people suddenly turned up at the Bangladeshi border, a mass exodus that is difficult to hide, that the world began to wake up.

As my Rohingya friends and I continue fighting for our cause from afar, we have only been able to look on as this extermination happens. We have witnessed Aung San Suu Kyi's sad betrayal of our people and of the idea of a Myanmar free of dictatorship, and we have seen the inaction of the international community. Our voices, our pens, and, most of all, social media are our only weapons.

The last time I heard from my brother Babuli, he was in China. Habibah and her husband fled to Bangladesh in August 2017. I have only been able to speak to them briefly on the phone and advise them to get as far away as possible from Bangladesh, where almost one million Rohingya now live with no hope of a future.

How many Rohingya still remain in Arakan today? Who can really say? Probably between 300,000 and 500,000 Muslims, counting both Rohingya and Kamans. The Rakhines and the army no longer differentiate between the two. Muslims are outlawed, and therefore all of us have to be exterminated. At least half of those still living in Arakan are in one of the many concentration camps. Others will be attempting to flee the country, hiding or trapped in forests surrounded by the army or Rakhines who are effectively starving them to death. Then there are the few remaining villages whose inhabitants live in fear because their turn will come.

It is November 2017 as I finish writing these lines. I continue my awareness-raising activities: I help to write and edit a blog and organise meetings to inform the world about what is happening as much as I can from Australia, I demonstrate. My father may not have survived, but my brother, sisters, and I are dispersed over several continents, stateless and rootless, while my mother remains in grave danger. She is my heartbeat and my blood. Not a day goes by that I don't think of her.

Today, our people are scattered. Rohingya are living in exile around the globe, but our hearts are more than ever in Arakan.

Afterword

In 2017, the world could no longer fail to notice the plight of the Rohingya in Myanmar, as hundreds of thousands fled their blazing homes and villages to neighbouring Bangladesh, or were slaughtered as they attempted to escape. The international community and the UN were finally forced to recognise this as genocide.

Yet the Rohingya had been trying to draw attention to this prolonged and increasingly violent persecution over many decades. My story is just the tip of the iceberg of the unimaginable suffering of many thousands of Rohingya like me. Our lives are precarious, whether in Myanmar, our native land, where many of us are in hiding or corralled into internal displacement camps, or in refugee camps in Bangladesh or forced exile in Malaysia, Thailand, and elsewhere. The Rohingya that have managed to escape alive remain, for the most part, stateless, illegal immigrants prey to human traffickers and vulnerable to arrest and torture.

In exile, my life hung by a thread. I barely survived the numerous arrests and tortures, and was unable to work to support myself or send much-needed funds back to my family in Myanmar. I could not explain this to my family without causing them worry; I did not want to add to their burden, nor for them to think that everywhere we went would dangerous for us as Rohingya. I knew this meant that they would think I was abandoning them and failing in my duty as the eldest son to support them. This led to many periods when I simply stopped contacting them because it was too painful. Causing family ruptures is one of the cruellest things that the Myanmar dictatorship has done.

The UNHCR's official recognition of the Rohingya as refugees was a ray of sunshine in the darkness. It revived in me my dreams of a university education, and becoming a lawyer, as my father had always hoped. Just illusions, in the end. After receiving my temporary protection letter, I travelled to the Muslim university in Malaysia to sign up for a course. But I was told that without a passport or money it would be impossible to enrol or apply for a grant. I had also long since given up marrying or starting a family, recognising that this, too, would be unimaginable in my situation.

I gradually came to the realisation that activism was my only solution; although I had no ambitions to become an activist, I couldn't stay silent about the truth. I still dreamt of studying and becoming part of society, but that dream was gradually fading as the years passed. Fate seemed to have other plans for me. So I decided to try to help my fellow Rohingya. I was aware of the risks, but I thought of the Chinese proverbs that my father had told me when I was a child: 'Without an organised society, men cannot become human' and 'The lamb that walks alone is easily attacked by the tiger'.

After making this decision while still in Malaysia, I spent as much time as I could in internet cafés studying international human rights treaties and reports. If I was not going to be able to access formal education, I had to be my own teacher and do everything in my power to pursue my education by other means. I wanted to cheat destiny.

After years of limited or no access to schooling, there is an estimated illiteracy rate of 90 per cent among the Rohingya. This, along with poverty, repression, and a lack of technology (most Rohingya live off-grid), is one of the reasons our voices have not been heard globally until now. Those of us with access to platforms like Facebook, and the literacy skills to use them, have had to counter the hatred and fake news coming out of Myanmar, and tell the world what is really happening to us: a genocide that had been going on for many years. Until now, we have been dependent on others to tell our story, and it has been highly risky, if not altogether forbidden, for journalists to enter Arakan and pursue real and free investigation without barriers and constraints. As Rohingya, we had been condemned to live in a world of suffering, from which no sound could escape.

In June 2012, I was well into my second year of prolonged detention in the Darwin immigration detention centre, Australia. I had not told my mother where I was, preferring her to be comforted by the thought that at least one of her children was free. But lying to her had become such torture for me that, with a heavy heart and suffering from depression, I finally decided to sever all contact with her. I felt it was better that my family did not depend on me, that they learnt to become self-sufficient. It was an agonising decision, all the more so as

I began to receive news of the large-scale massacres in Arakan that month.

I wrote in my diary:

Mum, I haven't contacted you because I can't give you what you need right now. I have been waiting to be released to be there for you. I did not want to abandon you. But now the genocide has accelerated ... I would give my life for you to be able to return to the miserable conditions you were in a few days ago, for you to survive this massacre ... Will you ever understand why your son was so far away from you when your life was in danger?

Overcome with impotent rage and despair, I punched the walls of my cell, choked with grief. I prayed for my family: 'Please let their hearts keep on beating. Please don't let their blood, the same blood that flows in my veins, be spilled in the Kaladan River. Please let them be saved by a miracle. Let the bloodbath pass them by.'

As I and the other Rohingya in the detention centre received calls from friends and family members trapped in Myanmar, crying for help down the lines of their illicit mobiles until the batteries ran out or they were slaughtered, we kept a detailed log of the pogroms and destruction.

One gut-wrenching appeal followed another:

'Brother! Their weapons are driven by their hatred. They sing in the streets, "This afternoon we're going to get rid of all the nigger villages ... Kill the niggers ..." Help us.'

'Send help. The international community — tell them to come —'

'The police and the Burmese army are on their side ...' The voice disintegrated into a hoarse rattle and was drowned out by tears, and then the line was cut.

'They're setting fire to the houses and shooting anyone who tries

to escape the blaze.'

'They've arrested the local NGO officials. We don't know what they've done with them.'

'They're looting our homes and raping the women.'

'Habib, I'm begging you! Tell the world. They're coming for us. They count us as less than animals. They've burnt our children in their very homes. There's nothing left of us.'

'Tell the world. I'm going to die. Why is the world allowing this barbarity to take place? Why aren't you telling them anything?'

'In their eyes, we're nothing but animals. They take our children, torture them, and then bury them with dozens of other bodies in mass graves ...'

'Our neighbours were burned alive. Pray to God for us, please. Pray to God to gather us to Him.'

The Myanmar authorities' official figures listed barely 130 dead, but we kept records of the villages and mosques burned to the ground and of the true number of deaths. Thousands of Rohingya died in the bloody summer of 2012. It was the start of five long years of uninterrupted genocide, during which Arakan State became a killing field.

However, at that precise moment, the world's gaze was turned elsewhere. Myanmar was opening up to democracy, by-elections were being held, and Aung San Suu Kyi was about to embark on a European tour less than two years after her release from house arrest. The world was transfixed.

For the army and the nationalist extremists, it was an auspicious moment. Murders, rapes, arrests, kidnappings, lootings, houses set ablaze, and mass graves were masked to the world by the joy of finally seeing the grande dame of democracy set free. My people disappeared in the euphoria of a new age of democracy in Myanmar. Genocide was a taboo word, and the

Rohingya, once again, did not exist.

The world was only listening to one voice in Myanmar, and at that critical moment the fate of the Rohingya depended on her. As long as that voice did not speak out, the massacre would continue. The world was at her feet. She had the power to denounce the horror and injustice, and call on the international community to intervene. She had the power to save lives. She was free, and the world was listening. She had the power to choose justice and tolerance, and show people what a democracy was. But Aung San Suu Kyi chose power.

As she gave her Nobel Peace Prize acceptance speech in Oslo on 16 June 2012, 150 Rohingya were massacred in Kiladang Village in Arakan State; the Burmese press wrote of eliminating the 'Bengali terrorists'; and the international press was still referring to an 'inter-ethnic conflict'.

The one voice of Myanmar had not spoken for us, and so now we would have to speak for ourselves.

Recommended Reading

Organisations

Amnesty International: https://www.amnesty.org/en/

Arakan Rohingya National Assembly (ARNA): http://arnauk.com

Arakan Rohingya National Organisation (ARNO): https://www.rohingya.
org/

Australian Burmese Rohingya Organization: http://abro.org.au/

Burma Campaign UK: https://burmacampaign.org.uk/

Burmese Rohingya Association in Japan: http://brajtokyo.blogspot.com/

Burmese Rohingya Association in Thailand: http://rohingyathai.blogspot.
com/

Chin Human Rights Organization (CHRO): www.chro.ca

Christian Solidarity Worldwide: https://www.csw.org.uk/

Fortify Rights: https://www.fortifyrights.org/

Free Rohingya Campaign (FRC): www.freerohingyacampaign.blogspot.
com/

Human Rights Watch: https://www.hrw.org/

Independent Mon News Agency: http://monnews.org/

International Committee of the Red Cross: https://www.icrc.org/en

Kaladan Press: http://www.kaladanpress.org/v3/

Karen News: http://karennews.org/

Khonumthung News: http://khonumthung.org/

Myanmar Ethnic Rohingya Human Rights Organisation: https://
merhrom.wordpress.com/

Myanmar Refugees: www.myanmarrefugees.blogspot.com/
Refugee Action Coalition Sydney: http://www.refugeeaction.org.au/
Refugees, Survivors and Ex-Detainees: http://riserefugee.org/
Reporters Without Borders: https://rsf.org/en
Rohingya Arakanese Refugee Committee: http://arrcinfo.blogspot.com/
Rohingya Blogger: www.rohingyablogger.com/
Tenaganita: http://www.tenaganita.net/
United Nations Human Rights Office of the High Commissioner:
    https://www.ohchr.org

News articles

'A letter from the roof of Darwin's Northern Immigration Detention
    Centre', Rohingya Arakanese Refugee Committee blog, 24 June 2011
'Case Study: Human trafficking of Bangladeshi and Rohingya boat
    people in Thailand', Human Rights at Sea website, 29 October 2014
'How Myanmar forces burned, looted and killed in a remote village',
    Reuters, 8 February 2018
'Revealed: how the Thai fishing industry trafficks, imprisons and
    enslaves', *The Guardian* online, 20 July 2015
'Rohingyan refugee pleads for Australia's permission to speak to EU',
    The Guardian online, 8 February 2018

Blogs

Arakan Diary: www.arakandiary.com (Habib's blog)
Dr Habib Siddqi: www.drhabibsiddiqui.blogspot.com
Maung Zarni: www.maungzarni.net
The Sail: www.thesail.wordpress.com
The Stateless: www.thestateless.com

Books

Ansel, Sophie and Garcia, Sam (2019), *Burmese Moons*. IDW publishing:
    California.
Constantine, Greg (2012), *Exiled to Nowhere: Burma's Rohingya*.

Nowhere People.

Ibrahim, Azeem (2018), *The Rohingyas: Inside Myanmar's Genocide*. Hurst Publishers: London.

Kritsanavarin, Suthep (2013), *Stateless Rohingya ... Running on Empty*. Regional Center for Social Science, Chiang Mai University: Chiang Mai.

McPherson, Poppy (2018), *The Shadows of Myanmar: Aung San Suu Kyi and the Persecution of the Rohingya*. I.B. Tauris: London.

Siddiqui, Habib (2019), *The Forgotten Rohingya: Their Struggle for Human Rights in Burma*.

Tenaganita (2008), *The Revolving Door*.

TV/film

Ghost Fleet, Shannon Service & Jeff Waldron

I Am Rohingya: A Genocide in Four Acts, Yusuf Zine

Refugees for Sale (Unreported World), Channel 4

Rohingya Vision, https://rohingyavision.com/

The Venerable W., Barbet Schroeder

'Why has a prominent Rohingya who found refuge in Melbourne been stopped from addressing European parliaments?', ABC (Australia)

Tributes and acknowledgements

As well as my own story, this is also the story of more than two million Rohingya across the world, and of a massacre that began in the 1960s and has continued unabated ever since. The story of every Rohingya man, woman, and child deserves to be told. These people, whose futures have been destroyed, are the first to whom I pay tribute.

I am grateful to all those who are committed to countering Burmese propaganda and exposing the reality of the conditions of the Rohingya in Arakan. There are many of them.

The first individual to whom I pay heartfelt tribute is the Burmese doctor and activist Maung Zarni who courageously and judiciously champions the Rohingya's rights. He is one of the few Bamars to have publicly opposed the lies, racism, and massacre of our people. I would also like to thank Graham Thom, Benjamin Zawacki, and Kavati, as well as Amnesty International, particularly in Australia and Malaysia, where they quickly alerted the international community and exerted pressure each time that I was arrested and detained. To Natalie Brinham, to the Australian MP Ronan Lee, to Joan Washington and Jane Black from the Red Cross, and to Chris Lewa, director of the Arakan Project.

Thank you to Phil Robertson and his organisation Human Rights

Watch; to Matthew Smith and Fortify Rights; and to Mark Farmaner and the courageous members of Burma Campaign UK; to Anna Robert and Benedict Rogers from Christian Solidarity Worldwide; and to the Burmese activists and politicians who respect Myanmar's minority groups. Their actions are vital to our survival.

My step-grandfather, the political activist Maung Kyaw Nu, who died on 31 May 2018, did a heroic and much-needed job for the Rohingya through the Burmese Rohingya Association in Thailand. He will be missed.

Thank you to Benjamin Ismaïl and Reporters Without Borders for their support. I would also like to pay tribute to the Rohingya leaders across the world who are working on behalf of their community. I hope they will not be offended if I do not name them all here.

I would also like to express my respect for friendly figures in the political and social spheres, in particular the comedian Zarganar.

In Malaysia, I met some extraordinary and unforgettable human rights activists who have helped thousands of Rohingya, including myself, to avoid far worse situations.

Thank you to the late Irène Fernandez and to her sister Aegile from the Tenaganita organisation. These two heroines risked their lives and consistently spoke out on behalf of Burmese migrants and refugees. These big-hearted women trusted and supported me in my most critical moments. I can never thank them enough.

Thank you to the human rights lawyers in Malaysia who defended us: Latifah Koya, MP YB Zuraidah, and Professor Kassim Azizah. Thank you to the journalists Mahi Ramakrishnan, Julia Zappei, Lt Kamarul, and Suthep Skritsanavarin, the first Thai reporter to investigate the Rohingya situation in the region and have the courage to take an interest in our daily lives. A huge thank you to him for his two visits to the Christmas Island detention centre and his letters of recommendation to the Australian Minister for Immigration. Thanks also to Greg Constantine and the amazing work he has done on our behalf. To the journalists Wa Lone and Kyaw Soe Oo from Reuters, who were arrested for attempting to reveal the truth about the mass graves in Arakan. I would also like to express my gratitude to Maung Kyaw Soe from Kaladan Press and to the Rohingya blogger U Ba Sein.

My thoughts are with the historians, writers, photographers, and others who have documented the history of the Rohingya, amongst whom are Maung Maung Tin, U Maung Maung Gyi, Maung Tan Lwin, A Tahir Ba Tha, Abu Anin, Satyendra Nath Ghoshal, Fayas Ahmed, Mohammed Yunus, Abid Bahar, Habib Siddiqui, Nafis Ahmed, Abdul Karim, Siddiq Khan, A.F.K. Jilani, Ashraf Alam, Zul Nurain, Gabriel Defert, General Sunthi (Thailand), and Zaw Min Htut, director of the Burmese Rohingya Association in Japan. To Abou Diaby.

Thank you to the people who have supported me in my private life. Their friendship, solidarity, and generosity have ensured my survival. They know who they are, and will always have a place in my heart.

I would like to pay particular tribute to Zafar Ahmed and to Abdul Gofor from the Myanmar Ethnic Rohingya Human Rights Organisation, and express my respect for Aung Naing, Sadek, and Kyaw Soe Aung of the National Democratic Party for Human Rights (in exile). Sadek founded the first school for refugee children in the Bangladesh camps as well as a school in Ampang Tasik in Malaysia.

My thoughts are with Harun, one of my oldest and most loyal friends, for whom I have infinite respect for his energetic promotion of understanding between different communities. He introduced me to Sophie and this book therefore owes him a great deal.

I cannot forget all the friends who have not hesitated to provide me with accommodation or help me financially particularly when I was in the hands of the human traffickers and my life depended on their willingness to help. They include Gurani, Hassan, Hla Myint, Kyaw Khin, Aesop, Alibai, Amin, Harun Rashid, and Yunus Bai.

My warmest thoughts go to my friend Faizal and to Khairul and his family who often put me up in their little room in Ampang Campuran between 2003 and 2005. Khairul died in 2009 when he was returning from work one evening in Penang, just a few months after his wife had died from cancer. They leave behind them three stateless orphans.

I would like to thank the activists for refugee rights who supported me during my prolonged detention in the Australian detention centres: Justine Davis, Carl O'Connor, Pamela Curr and Emma Murphy in Darwin, Ian Rintoul from the Refugee Action Coalition Sydney, Michele Lobo in Melbourne, Jennifer Scott from the Australian Red Cross, and

Kate Coddington in the United States. Their support helped me to stay strong. Thanks also to Adam Tel, Madhuni and Ramesh (RISE refugees organisation), and Russell Mall (Rohingya Action Group).

My deepest gratitude goes to the lawyers who defend the rights of refugees in prolonged detention: Koulla Roses in particular, and of course John B. Lawrence from the John Toohey Chamber. Thank you to my lawyer, Sanmati Verma.

Thank you to Jamal Ikazban and Faouzia Bensalem.

My special thanks to my publishers, Bertil Scali, Jeanne Pois-Fournier, and Marie Leroy from Éditions de La Martinière who have given the Rohingya a space for their voices and their story to be heard. And to my English-language publishers, Scribe, in particular Henry Rosenbloom, Bridie Riordan, and Molly Slight, and my English translator, Andrea Reece, for making a part of the Rohingya history known.

To Sophie.
To my family.
Habib